THE YES OF JESUS CHRIST

THE YES OF JESUS CHRIST

Exercises in Faith, Hope, and Love

POPE BENEDICT XVI

(Joseph Ratzinger)

Translated by Robert Nowell

A Crossroad Book
Crossroad Publishing Company
New York

The Crossroad Publishing Company
481 Eighth Avenue, Suite 1550, New York, NY 10001

Originally published as *Aus Christus Schauen: Einübung in Glaube,
Hoffnung, Liebe.* Copyright © 1989 Verlag Herder, Freiburg im
Breisgau.

English translation copyright © 1991 by The Crossroad
Publishing Company.

Formerly published in hardcover as *To Look on Christ* by
The Crossroad Publishing Company in 1991.

Printed in the United States of America

Library of Congress Cataloging-in-Publication Data is available

ISBN 0-8245-2374-1

1   2   3   4   5   6   7   8   9   10   09   08   07   06   05

Dedicated in gratitude and admiration
to Josef Pieper
on his 85th birthday

CONTENTS

I. FAITH — 3

Faith as a Fundamental Human Attitude
in Everyday Life — 5

Is Agnosticism a Solution? — 9

Interlude: The Foolishness of the Wise and
the Conditions for True Wisdom — 13

Natural Knowledge of God — 21

"Supernatural" Faith and Its Foundations — 27

Developing the First Stages — 30

2. HOPE — 39

The Optimism of the Modern Age
and Christian Hope — 39

Three Biblical Examples of the Nature
of Christian Hope — 49

Bonaventure and Thomas Aquinas
on Christian Hope — 64

3. HOPE AND LOVE   69

Hope and Love in the Mirror of
    Their Antitheses   69
The Essential Nature of Love   88
The Nature and Way of *Agape*   IOI
A Saying from the Sermon on the Mount   IO5

EPILOGUE: TWO SERMONS ON
    FAITH AND LOVE   IO9

"What Shall I Do to Inherit Eternal Life?"
    A Homily on Luke 10:25–37   IO9
The Pure Vision and the Right Way:
    A Sermon for the Feast of St. Henry   II5

NOTES   I23

PREFACE TO THE ORIGINAL EDITION   I33

THE YES OF JESUS CHRIST

· 1 ·

FAITH

THE REFLECTIONS THIS BOOK offers are not concerned primarily with thinking theories through. Their aim is to invite the reader to "spiritual exercises." What in fact are these? What do they involve us in doing? One can only exercise or practice something one already somehow possesses: it presupposes a pre-existing foundation. But it is only through practicing it that its relevant quality becomes my own so that I have it at my disposal and it becomes fruitful. A pianist has to practice his or her skill, otherwise it becomes lost. Athletes have to train: it is the only way of reaching the summit of their actual ability. After I have broken my leg I must practice using the affected limb again so that it regains all its old functions. What are we trying to practice during this retreat? Spiritual exercises are practice in being a Christian, practicing living on the basis of faith. But because being a Christian does not mean some special skill alongside other skills but simply the correct living out of being human, we could also say that we want to practice the skill of living correctly: we want to learn better the skill of skills, the art of being human.

Here we need to look at one aspect of our life. In our contemporary society there is a highly developed system of vocational and technical training that has increased to the utmost the possibilities of human mastery over material things. Human ability in the sense of dominating the world has reached dizzy heights. In doing things we have become very great, but when it comes to being, to the art of existence, things look very different indeed. We know what can be done with things and people, but what things and people are is something we do not talk about any longer. What we shall be concerned about in these coming days is this lost art of being able to live. In this matter we find ourselves in the same kind of situation as after a kind of multiple fracture: we must gradually learn again how to "move" in faith, how to use all our inner powers. In this context talks and lectures can only be a kind of introductory lesson, a first impetus toward a personal and social inner commitment and effort—which is above all what it all depends on if these exercises are to be fruitful.

Faith is the fundamental act of Christian existence. In the act of faith the essential structure of Christianity is expressed, its answer to the question how in the art of being human one can reach the goal. There are other answers. Not all religions are "faith." Buddhism in its classic form, for example, does not aim at this act of self-transcendence, of encounter with the totally other—with God, who addresses me and invites me to love. Characteristic of Buddhism is rather a kind of radical internalization: an act of climbing not out of oneself but into oneself, an act that is meant to lead to liberation from the yoke of individuality, from the burden of being a person, and to a return into the common identity of all being that, in comparison with our experience of existence, can be described as not-being, as nothing, in order to express its total otherness.[1]

Faith as a Fundamental Human Attitude in Everyday Life

Here it is not our aim to get embroiled in this dispute, though much of what is to be said in these talks could well be a silent answer to the questions that it raises. What we are concerned about is quite simply to learn better the fundamental act of being a Christian, the act of faith. If we take this path we run at once into an obstacle. We become aware, as it were, of one of our internal fractures that hinder our movement in the field of faith. The question arises: is faith an attitude worthy of a modern and mature human being? "Faith" seems to us something temporary and provisional that one ought really to be able to get beyond, even if frequently it is unavoidable precisely as a provisional attitude: nobody can actually know and master from his or her own knowledge and understanding all that in a technological civilization our life depends on. Very many things—in fact by far the most of them—we have to accept with trust in "science," especially as this seems sufficiently confirmed for the individual on the basis of common experience. Every day from dawn to dusk we all use products of technology the scientific basis of which we do not know. Who is capable of checking and making sure of the structural engineering of a skyscraper? the working of the elevator? the whole world of electric and electronic apparatus we have to deal with? or (where it gets trickier) the reliability of the composition of a medicine? One could go on and on. We live in a network of things we do not know about but that we rely on because our experience of them is in general positive. We "believe" that all this will be okay, and through this kind of "faith" we are able to have a share and interest in the product of other people's knowledge.

What kind of faith is this then that unconsciously we are practicing all the time and that indeed is the foundation of our everyday coexistence? Instead of starting off by trying to produce a definition let us stick with what can be established directly. Two contrasting aspects of this kind of "faith" leap to the eye. First of all we could establish that some kind of faith of this kind is indispensable for our life. To begin with this is quite simply because otherwise nothing would work any more: everyone would have to start from scratch all the time. More profoundly this applies in the sense that human life becomes impossible if one can no longer trust other people and is no longer able to rely on their experience, on their knowledge, on what is already provided for us. That is one aspect of this "faith," the positive side. On the other side it is naturally the expression of a lack of knowledge and to that extent of an attitude of inferiority: it would be better to know. Most people can only rely on the entire mechanism of the technological world because some people are there who have gone into the matter and know all about it. To this extent the desire to move as far as possible from faith to knowledge is right and proper, at least in this context. Although we are still a long way from the domain of what is religious and are moving in the sphere of coping with life in a purely this-worldly, everyday manner, we have nevertheless gained insights that are of importance for the phenomenon of religious faith and that for that reason we would like explicitly to emphasize once again.

We said that two different aspects are to be differentiated in the framework of what we would like to label "everyday faith." First of all it bears the character of what is insufficient and provisional: it is a purely initial preliminary stage of knowledge that whenever possible one will strive to pass beyond. But alongside this there is something quite different: this kind of "faith" is a mutual trust, a common sharing in understanding and in master-

ing the world, and this aspect is essential for the organization of human life. A society without trust cannot live.
The phrase that Thomas Aquinas coined for a different
context applies here too: for human beings lack of faith
goes against nature.[2] This also brings home to us that the
different contexts and levels of human life are not completely disconnected.

With this we have worked out something like an
"axiological structure" of natural faith: that is, we have
investigated those aspects of it that relate to its value and
have discovered that on the one hand this kind of faith
contains a minus value with regard to "knowledge" but
that on the other hand it includes a fundamental value of
human existence without which no society would exist. In
addition we can now label the individual elements that
belong to this kind of faith—its "existential structure."
There are three. This kind of faith is always directed
towards someone who "knows" the matter in hand. It
presupposes the genuine expertise of qualified and trust-
worthy people. The second element is the trust of the
majority who in their daily use of things are able to build
less on the substantial knowledge that should lie behind
such use. And finally the third element is a certain verification of knowledge in everyday experience. I may not be
able to demonstrate scientifically that the electric current
is working okay, but this is shown me by the everyday
functioning of my various pieces of electrical apparatus,

so that even though I am not a scientific specialist in this field I am not operating in the field of pure "faith" that is totally lacking in confirmation.

Is Agnosticism a Solution?

In all this we catch glimpses of religious faith, and similarities of structure become visible. But if we now try to make the transition to religious faith, the way is immediately blocked by a weighty objection that could be formulated more or less as follows. It could well be that in human interaction it would be impossible for everyone to "know" everything that is essential and useful for life and that our ability to act therefore rests on our sharing in others' "knowledge" through our "faith." Nevertheless in all this we remain in the field of human knowledge that in principle everyone is capable of acquiring. But on the other hand with the faith that involves revelation we cross the boundary of specifically human knowledge. Even if the existence of God could perhaps be included under the heading of "knowledge," revelation and its contents remain "faith" for everyone, something beyond what is accessible to our knowledge. Here there is no reference to the specialized knowledge of a few on which we can rely because they know things directly from their own research. Thus we are now faced once again with the question: is this kind of faith compatible with modern critical awareness? Would it not be more fitting for the mature man or woman of our age to refrain from a judgment on matters of this kind and to await the moment when science will hold in its hand definite answers even to this range of questions? The attitude expressed in such questions corresponds without a doubt to the average academic conviction of today: the honesty of ratiocination and humility in the face of the unknown seem to recommend agnosticism, while explicit atheism already knows too much and clearly contains a dogmatic element within itself. Nobody can claim that he or she "knows" in the proper sense of that word that there is no God. One can work with the hypothesis that God does not exist and try on that basis to explain the universe. That fundamentally is the sign under which the modern natural sciences stand. When their method respects its boundaries it remains clear that the realm of the hypothetical cannot be transcended and that even an apparently consistent explanation of the universe does not lead to a scientific certainty about the nonexistence of God. Nobody can grasp experimentally the totality of being and its requirements. At this point we reach quite simply the limits of *la condition humaine*—of the human ability to know as such; and this not just under the conditions of today but essentially and insurpassably. Of its nature the question of God cannot be squeezed within the boundaries of scientific research in the strict sense of the term. In this sense the claim of "scientific atheism" is an absurd presumption, yesterday just as much as today and tomorrow. But all the more we are forced to face up to whether the question of God does not simply surpass the boundaries of human ability so that to this extent agnosticism would be the only correct attitude for men and women: in keeping with the nature of being, honest, indeed in the profoundest sense of the word "pious"—the recognition of where our grasp and vision end, respect for what has not been disclosed to us. Ought it perhaps to be the new piety of human thinking to leave what cannot be investigated and be content with what we are given?

Anyone who wishes to answer this as a believer must beware of any rashness. But this kind of humility and piety immediately raises the objection that the thirst for the infinite belongs quite simply to essential human nature and is indeed precisely that essential nature. The human frontier can only be that which has no frontiers, and the boundaries of science ought not to be confused with the boundaries of our existence. That would be to misunderstand both science and humankind. When science raises the claim that it exhausts the boundaries of human knowledge it lands itself in the realm of the unscientific. All this seems to me to be true but, as I have already said, too hasty and rash as an answer at this point. We should rather patiently examine the hypothesis of agnosticism from the point of view of its viability—in the sense of whether it can be a viable enduring answer not just on the part of science but on the part of human life. Thus the right question to be put to agnosticism is whether its proposal is capable of realization. As human beings can we simply leave the question of God on one side—the question of where we come from, where we are going, and the measure of our being? Can we simply live hypothetically "as if there were no God" even if perhaps there is? For human beings the question of God is not some theoretical problem like, for example, the question whether there are as yet unknown elements outside the periodic table and others of this kind. On the contrary, the question of God is an eminently practical affair that has its effects on all spheres of our life. If therefore I allow agnosticism to be valid in theory, in practice I must nevertheless decide between two possibilities: to live as if there were no God or to live as if God did exist and was the determining reality for my life. If I adopt the first choice, I have in practice taken up an atheist position and made the basis of my entire life a possibly false hypothesis. If I decide for the second option I am acting once again within a purely subjective religiosity that might remind one of Pascal, whose entire philosophical struggle at the start of the modern age centered on this complex of intellectual issues. Because he reached the conviction that the question could not actually be solved by ratiocination alone, he recommended the agnostic to plump for the second choice and to live as if God existed. The agnostic would then in the course of the experiment and only as a result of this come to the awareness of having made the right choice.[3] However this may be, the attractiveness of the agnostic solution quite clearly does not stand up to closer examination. As a pure theory it seems extremely plausible, but of its nature agnosticism is more than a theory: how one lives life in practice is in question. And when one tries to "practice" it in what is thus its true extent it slips away like a soap bubble: it collapses because the choice it would like to avoid cannot be evaded. We are not allowed neutrality when faced with the question of God. We can only say yes or no, and this with all the consequences extending right down to the smallest details of life.

Interlude: The Foolishness of the Wise and the Conditions for True Wisdom

At this point I would like to interrupt a train of argument that has perhaps become somewhat abstract and insert a biblical parable, after which we shall have to pick up the threads of our discourse once again. I am thinking of the story told by Jesus that is recorded in Luke 12:16–23:

The land of a rich man brought forth plentifully; and he thought to himself, "What shall I do, for I have nowhere to store my crops?" And he said, "I will do this: I will pull down my barns, and build larger ones; and there I will store all my grain and my goods. And I will say to my soul, 'Soul, you have ample goods laid up for many years; take your ease, eat, drink, be merry.'" But God said to him, "Fool! This night your soul is required of you; and the things you have prepared, whose will they be?" So is he who lays up treasure for himself, and is not rich toward God.

The rich man of this parable was without a doubt intelligent: he certainly knew his business. He knew how to weigh up the opportunities of the market: he took sufficient account of the uncertainties both of nature and of human behavior. He is cautious in his calculations, and success proves him right. If we might expand this parable a little, we could say that this man was certainly much too canny to be an atheist. But he lived as an agnostic, "as if God did not exist." That kind of man does not bother himself with such uncertain things as the existence of a God. He is concerned with what is certain, what can be calculated. Hence his aims in life are very much of this world, very tangible: affluence and the happiness of doing well. But then there occurs precisely what he had not taken into account: God speaks to him and tells him of an eventuality that he had excluded from his calculations as being too uncertain and too unimportant—what becomes of his soul when it stands naked before God, beyond all possession and success. "This night your soul is required of you." The man whom everyone knew as intelligent and successful is in God's eyes an idiot: "Fool!" he says to him, and in the sight of reality he now appears with all his calculations as remarkably foolish and shortsighted, for in all his calculations he had forgotten the reality—that his soul did not only want possession and gratification but would stand before God.

This clever man who is a fool strikes me as a very exact picture of our average modern attitude. Our technical and economic capabilities have grown to an extent that could not have been imagined earlier. The precision of our calculations is worthy of admiration. Despite all the ghastly things that have happened in this age of ours the opinion is continually becoming stronger among many people that we are now close to the point of bringing about the greatest happiness of the greatest number and finally ushering in a new phase of history, a civilization of humanity, in which at last all will be able to eat and drink their fill and all can enjoy themselves to their heart's content. But precisely when we seem to be coming close to humankind's redemption of itself, frightening explosions erupt from the depths of the unsatisfied and oppressed human soul to tell us: "Fool, you have forgotten yourself, your soul and its unquenchable thirst—its longing for God." The agnosticism of our age that seems so reasonable, that lets God be God in order to turn human beings into human beings, turns out to be shortsighted foolishness. The aim of our exercises, however, ought to be to hearken to what God has to say, to listen to the call of our soul, once more to discover in its depths the mystery of God.

Let us stay for a few more moments within the perspectives opened up by this train of thought before picking up once again the threads of our earlier discourse. Man's stretching out toward God, the quest for the creative ground of all things, is something very different from precritical or uncritical thinking. On the contrary: rejecting the question of God, renouncing this supreme human openness, is an act of shutting oneself in on oneself; it is to forget the inner call of our being. In this context Josef Pieper has cited Cardinal Newman's adaptation of some lines of Hesiod that express this fact with inimitable elegance and precision: "Best of all is he who is wise by his own wit; next best he who is wise by the wit of others; but whoso is neither able to see nor willing to hear, he is a good-for-nothing fellow."[4] Pointing in the same direction is what Newman himself has to say about the fundamental relationship of human beings to truth. All too often people are inclined, the great theologian states, to wait quietly as if proofs of the reality of revelation would walk in through their front door, as if they were in the position of judges rather than suppliants. "Like this is the conduct of those who resolve to treat the Almighty with dispassionateness, a judicial temper, clear-headedness and candor." But we deceive ourselves by making ourselves the lord of truth in this way. It withdraws itself from those who claim self-sufficiency and reveals itself only to those who approach it in an attitude of reverence, of adoring humility.[5]

"He has put down the mighty from their thrones, and exalted those of low degree"—these words from the Magnificat come to mind, and perhaps this is precisely the perspective in which they can be understood. For they do not contain an anticipation of the class struggle; rather they express the amazement of someone moved and affected by God at God's ways. So what is brought to light in them is something fundamental. It is not a question of political changes, at least not in the first instance: it is a question of human dignity, its loss and its recovery. Those who make themselves lords of truth and end by leaving truth on one side when it does not allow itself to be dominated ultimately place power above truth. Their criterion becomes power, ability. But precisely in this way they lose themselves: the throne on which they place themselves is a false throne; what they think is ascending the throne is in reality their fall.

Perhaps this sounds too apocalyptic, too theological.

It will come down to earth if we consider the pattern of thought of the modern age in more detail. The starting point of the modern natural sciences is that human beings, as Galileo put it, put nature on the rack by means of experiment and thus extract from nature the secrets that it will not voluntarily reveal. This method has certainly brought to light things that are important and beneficial to all of us. We have learned all the things that can be done with nature.[6] The significance of this knowledge and of the ability that has been attained in this way should not be belittled. The only thing is that, if we grant validity to this way of thinking alone, the throne of domination over nature on which we have placed ourselves will have been built on nothing: it must collapse and bring us and the world down in its fall. To be able to do and make is one thing, to be able to be another: being able to do and make is no use if we do not know what it is for, if we no longer ask who we are and what the truth of things is. The isolation of the knowledge of mastery is the very throne of pride whose fall follows inevitably from its lack of foundations. If what ultimately counts is only that knowledge that finally identifies itself through being able to do and make, then we are shortsighted fools who are building without any foundations. We have then elevated "power" to become the unique criterion and betrayed our proper vocation, the truth. The wisdom of pride becomes sheer

folly. To a "critical" way of thinking that criticizes everything except human beings themselves we thus oppose
openness to the infinite, vigilance, and sensitivity for the
whole of being: a humility of thought that is ready to
bow before the majesty of truth, before which we are not
judges but suppliants—it reveals itself only to the watchful and humble heart. If it is already true that the great
discoveries of science reveal themselves only to long,
watchful, and patient labor that is ready always to correct
itself and let itself be taught, then it is self-evident that
the highest truths demand a humble and continuous
readiness to listen. "He has exalted those of low degree":
this is no more an expression of primitive moralism than
it is a slogan of the class struggle. What it is concerned
with is fundamental human attitudes. It is only to a
humble willingness to listen and learn that does not let
itself be discouraged by any refusal, nor be led astray
either by applause or rejection, nor even by the devices
and desires of our own hearts—it is only to this humility of thought that the majesty of truth reveals itself and
thereby grants access to our true dimension. This kind of
openness to the infinite and to the One who is infinite
has nothing to do with credulity: on the contrary, it
demands the keenest self-criticism. It is more open and
more critical than that limitation to the sphere of the
empirical in which human beings make their desire for
mastery the final criterion of knowledge.

All this shows us the attitudes we need to set against an unassuming agnosticism because it is only they that correspond to the unavoidability of the question of God: alertness for the deeper dimensions of reality; asking about the totality of our human existence and of reality in general; humility in front of the greatness of truth; and readiness to be purified by and for it. Later it will become evident that we need to include yet another factor that has not yet been mentioned: just as in empirical matters we begin with a kind of faith and need the witness of those who know in order to attain knowledge ourselves, so too in this difficult and at the same time decisive sector of our awareness we need to be ready to listen to the great witnesses to the truth, to the witnesses of God, and to allow ourselves to be led by them in order to follow the path of knowledge. Furthermore, just as every science and every art require persistence and practice, things cannot be different in approaching God. The organs with which we perceive truth can become dulled to the point of complete blindness and deafness. Pius XII already gave a warning of this kind against losing one's sense of God, and Pope John Paul II has repeated this warning.[7] In this context the Fathers of the Church have continually referred to Christ's saying: "Blessed are the pure in heart, for they shall see God" (Matt. 5:8). The "pure" heart is the one that is open and humble. The impure heart according to this is the opposite, the presumptuous heart that is shut in on itself, that is completely filled up with itself and incapable of finding room for the majesty of truth that demands reverence and ultimately worship.

At this point, before picking up the threads of our earlier discourse, let us briefly summarize the results that have emerged from this anthropological interlude. We said that the question of God is unavoidable and does not admit of abstention. In order to approach it certain fundamental virtues are essential, which are as it were its methodological presuppositions: listening to the message that rises up from our existence and from the world as a whole; attentiveness towards humankind's religious perception and experience; the resolute and unwavering commitment of our time and inner energy to this question that affects everyone personally.

Natural Knowledge of God

The question now arises: is there an answer to this? And if there is, what kind of certainty can we expect? In his epistle to the Romans the apostle Paul found himself confronted with precisely this complex of problems: he answered with a philosophical reflection based on the facts of religious history. In the megalopolis of Rome, the Babylon of that age, he encountered that type of moral decadence that rested on the complete loss of tradition, on being cut off from that inner evidence that had once provided people with their customs and rules of behavior. Nothing is self-evident any longer, everything is possible and nothing impossible. No value holds any longer, no norm is sacrosanct. All that counts is the ego and the moment. Traditional religions are merely façades with no support from within: what remains is naked cynicism.

The answer the apostle gives to this metaphysical and moral cynicism of a decadent society ruled only by the law of power is astonishing. He claims that in reality they know very well about God: "What can be known about God is plain to them, because God has shown it to them" (Rom. 1:19). He justifies this claim as follows: "Ever since the creation of the world his invisible nature, namely, his eternal power and deity, has been clearly perceived in the things that have been made" (Rom. 1:20). From this Paul draws the conclusion: "So they are without excuse" (ibid.). Truth was available to them but they did not want it nor the claim it would make on them. The apostle talks of the "wickedness of men who by their wickedness suppress the truth" (Rom. 1:18). Human beings oppose the truth that would demand submission of them—submission in the form of honoring God and giving God thanks (Rom. 1:21). For Paul the moral collapse of society is merely the logical consequence and the exact mirror-image of this fundamental perversion. When we place our own will, our pride, and our comfort above the claim of truth, everything is in the end necessarily turned upside down: it is not God to whom worship is due that is worshipped any longer; what are worshipped are the images, the appearance, the prevailing opinion that wins domination over people. This general perversion extends to all fields of life. What is unnatural becomes normal: the person who lives against truth also lives against nature. People's powers of invention no longer serve what is good but the ingenuity and refinement of evil. The relationship between man and wife, between parents and children is dissolved, and in this way the sources of life are blocked up. It is no longer life that reigns but death, and a civilization of death has become established (Rom. 1:21–32).

Here Paul has drawn a picture of decadence that strikes the contemporary reader as alarmingly topical. But he is not content merely to describe, as is the custom in such times: a rather perverse form of moralism that remains self-indulgently negative in its condemnations. The apostle's analysis on the other hand leads to diagnosis and thus becomes a challenge: at the start of the whole thing stands the rejection of truth in favor of comfort or, as we would say, utility. The starting point is resistance to the evidence laid down in human beings for the creator who is concerned for them and summons them. For Paul atheism, or agnosticism lived in an atheist manner, is no innocent affair. For him it always rests on resistance to a perception that is in itself open to human beings but whose requirements they refuse to accept. We are not condemned to ignorance with regard to God. We can "see" God if we hearken to the voice of our essential nature, to the voice of creation, and let ourselves be led by this. The purely idealistic atheist is beyond Paul's ken.

What should one say to this? The apostle is here clearly alluding to the opposition between philosophy and religion in the ancient world. Greek philosophy had reached the point of recognizing the one spiritual foundation of the world, the only thing that deserved the name of God even if in forms that were contradictory and individually inadequate. But its efforts at the critique of religion were soon hampered, and despite this fundamental character it was more and more obliged to devote itself to the justification of worshipping both a pantheon of gods and the power of the state. The "suppression of truth" was obvious.[8] To this extent Paul's diagnosis is very well founded for the actual historical situation with which he had to deal. But does what he has to say apply beyond this limited historical context? Certainly it will need modification in detail, but in its essence it describes not just an accidental slice of history but the persistent situation of humankind, of human beings before God. The history of religion is coextensive with the history of humankind.

As far as we can see, there has never been a time when the question about the wholly other, the divine, has been alien to human beings.

There has always been a knowledge about God. And throughout the history of religion we encounter, often in different guises, the remarkable division between knowledge of the one God and turning towards other powers that are seen as more dangerous, closer, and hence more important for men and women than the mysterious distant God. The whole of history is marked by this strange dilemma between the silent, gentle claim of truth and the urgent pressure of utility, of getting on with the powers that mould the everyday world. And always there is this victory of utility over truth, even though the trace of truth and its own power is never completely lost and often survives in shifting forms in a jungle full of poisonous plants.

Does this apply today, in a completely nonreligious culture, in the culture of rationality and its technological application? I think it does. Even today human questioning reaches inevitably beyond the sphere of technological rationality. Even today we ask not only: "What can I make?" but also: "What must I do?" and: "Who am I?" There are of course evolutionary cosmologies that elevate the nonexistence of God to the level of rational evidence and thus aim at proving that the truth is precisely that there is no God. But the mythological character of such efforts at a comprehensive understanding is obvious when it comes to the essential points. The immense gaps in our knowledge are papered over by mythological constructs whose apparent rationality cannot seriously deceive anyone.[9] That the rationality of the world cannot be sensibly and usefully explained on the basis of irrationality is evident. And thus the logos at the origin of all things remains as it always was the best hypothesis, and one that indeed demands of us that we should give up the gestures of domination and adopt those of humble receptivity. The silent evidence for God has not, even today, been submerged, though it has probably been more obstructed than ever through the violence exerted on us by power and utility.

Thus the situation today is characterized fundamentally by the same tension between two opposed tendencies that runs through the whole of history: the inner openness for God of the human soul on the one hand, and on the other the stronger force of immediate needs and experiences. We are torn hither and thither between the two. We cannot break away from God, but neither do we have the strength to break through to God: with our own resources we cannot build the bridges that would lead to a definite relationship with this God. Thus one can always say with Thomas that unbelief is unnatural, but at the same time it is always true that human beings cannot completely dispel the strange twilight that hangs over the question of the eternal, that God must cross over to them and talk to them if real relations are to be established with him.[10]

"Supernatural" Faith and Its Foundations

But how should this happen? This question now leads us back to the considerations we began with about the structure of faith. The answer runs: God's speaking to us reaches us through men and women who have listened to God and come into contact with God; through men and women for whom God has become an actual experience and who as it were know him at first hand. To understand this we must consider the structure of knowledge and faith we worked out earlier. Then we said that attached to faith on the one hand was the aspect of knowledge that is not self-sufficient, while on the other hand there is the aspect of mutual trust whereby another's knowledge becomes mine. The element of trust thus bears in itself at the same time the element of sharing: through my trust I come to share in another's knowledge. Here is to be found what might be termed the social aspect of the phenomenon of faith. Nobody knows everything, but together we know what is needful: faith forms a network of mutual dependence that is at the same time a network of mutual solidarity, of supporting oneself and being supported. This fundamental anthropological structure recurs in our relationship to God: indeed, it is here that it has its primary form and the center that holds it together. Our knowledge of God, too, depends on this mutuality, on a trust that becomes sharing and is then verified for the individual in his or her lived experience. Our relationship with God is first of all and at the same time also a relationship with our fellow men and women: it rests on a communion of human beings, and indeed the communication of relationship with God mediates the deepest possibility of human communication that goes beyond utility to reach the ground of the person.

Admittedly, in order to be able to receive as my own in communication this knowledge of someone else and to experience its proof in my own life, I must myself be open to God. It is only if the perception is present in me that the sound of the eternal can reach me through someone else. To this extent sharing in knowledge of God through another person is more personal than sharing in knowledge with a technical specialist. The knowledge of God demands inner watchfulness, interiorization, a heart that is open and that in silent composure becomes personally aware of its direct links with its creator. But at the same time it is true that God does not reveal himself to the isolated ego and excludes individualistic isolation: being related to God is tied up with being related to our brothers and sisters, with communion with them.

At this point an unexpected step is disclosed. The "natural faith" whereby we rely on results that we cannot test for ourselves finds its justification, we said, in the knowledge of the individuals who know the matter in hand and have tested it. This kind of faith remains faith for the individual but refers to the perception of someone else. In our first approach to the religious question it seemed to us that it was precisely this decisive element that was lacking in supernatural, religious faith: here apparently there is no one with actual perception but all seem to be merely believers, and this appeared to us as the problematic point in religious faith. But now we have to say that things are not in fact so. In supernatural faith too the many live on the few and the few live for the many. Even in the matter of God we are not all blind people tapping our way along in the dark. Here too there are those to whom perception has been vouchsafed: "Your father Abraham rejoiced that he was to see my day; he saw it and was glad," said Christ of Israel's progenitor (John 8:56). In the midst of history he himself stands as the great seer, and all his sayings spring from this immediate contact with the Father. "He who has seen me has seen the Father" (John 14:9) applies to all of us.

Of its essence Christian faith is sharing in the vision of Jesus, mediated by his word, which is the authentic expression of his vision. Jesus' vision is the point of reference of our faith, the point where it is anchored in reality.

Developing the First Stages

This fundamental statement includes a series of percep-
tions that I would like to develop briefly.

Anchoring Faith in the Vision
of Jesus and of the Saints

Jesus, who knows God at first hand and sees God, is for
that reason the true mediator between God and human
beings. His human vision of the divine reality is the
source of light for everyone. But even Jesus should not
simply be considered in isolation, pushed away into a distant historical past. We have already mentioned Abraham:
now we must add that the light of Jesus is reflected in the
saints and shines out again from them. "Saints," however,
are not just those canonized by name. There are always
hidden saints who in their fellowship with Jesus receive a
ray of his brightness, actual and real experience of God.
Perhaps in order to make this more exact we should pick
up a remarkable saying used by the Old Testament in connection with the story of Moses: if they cannot see God
full in the face they do nevertheless see God, they at least
see God's back (Exod. 33:23).[11] And just as Moses' face

shone after this encounter with God, so the light of Jesus shines from the life of men and women of this kind.

Thomas Aquinas indeed developed the scientific character of theology from this state of affairs. He pointed out that (according to Aristotle) all sciences are related to each other in a system of mutual justification and dependence. No one science provides a rational justification for and reflects the whole: each presupposes at some point rational foundations established by another science. Only *one* science, following Aristotle, penetrates to the real foundation of all human knowledge: hence he called this the "first philosophy." All the others presuppose at least these fundamental reflections and for this reason are *scientiae subalternae,* subordinate sciences building on the work of one or more of the others.

Into this general theory of science Thomas inserts his explanation of theology. He says that in this sense theology too is a "subordinate science," which does not itself "see" and "prove" its ultimate rational foundations. It is as it were suspended from the "knowledge of the saints," from their vision: this vision is the point of reference of theological thought that guarantees its legitimacy. In this sense the work of the theologian is always "secondary" relative to the real experience of the saints. Without this point of reference, without this inmost anchoring in such experience, it loses its character of reality. That is the humility that is imposed on the theologian. . . . Theology becomes an empty intellectual game and loses its scientific character without the realism of the saints, without their contact with the reality it is all about.[12]

The Verification of Faith in Life

If we entrust ourselves to the vision of Jesus and have faith in what he says, this does not in any way mean we are moving into complete darkness. Jesus' message answers to an inner expectation of our heart: it corresponds to an inner light of our being that stretches out towards the truth of God. Of course, at first we are believers "at second hand." But Thomas Aquinas rightly characterizes faith as a process, an inner way, when he says: "The light of faith makes one see what is believed."[13] In his Gospel John often indicates this process, for example in the story of Jesus and the Samaritan woman. The woman tells people about what happened to her with Jesus and tells them that in him she has recognized the Messiah—the bringer of salvation who opens up the way to God and thus the knowledge that gives life. The fact that it is this woman who is saying this makes her fellow citizens sit up and take notice: they believe in Jesus "because of the woman's testimony"—they believe at second hand. But because this was so they invited Jesus to stay with them, and thus they entered into conversation with him. Eventually they could say to the woman: "It is no longer because of your words that we believed, for we have heard for ourselves, and we *know* that this is indeed the Savior of the world" (John 4:42). In the living encounter faith has become recognition, has become "knowledge."

Admittedly it would be deceptive now to think of the way of faith as progress in a straight line. Because it is so closely connected with our life that moves up and down in all sorts of ways, there are always setbacks that require a new start. Every stage of life must find its own maturity and can fall into its own particular immaturity. Nevertheless we can say, however, that in the life of faith a certain evidence of this faith is growing: its reality affects us, and the experience of a life lived in faith verifies the fact for us that Jesus is indeed the savior of the world.

At this point the second aspect we mentioned is linked with the first. In the New Testament the word "saint" was a general description for Christians, who even at that time probably did not all have the qualities demanded of a canonized saint. But this terminology expressed the fact that they were all called to use their experience of the risen Lord to become a point of reference for others that could bring them into contact with Jesus' vision of the living God. This applies just as much today. Believers who let themselves be formed and led by the faith of the

Church should in all their weaknesses and difficulties be windows for the light of the living God; and if they truly believe, this is what they are. The believer should be a countervailing force against the powers that suppress the truth, against this wall of prejudice that blocks our view of God. Faith that is just beginning ought as it were to be able to lean on that kind of person. Just as the Samaritan woman became the occasion of an invitation to Jesus, so the faith of those who believe is a point of reference for the search for God in the darkness of a world that is largely opposed to God.

In this connection it is of interest to recall that after the end of the apostolic age the early Church had as yet developed only relatively little in the way of direct missionary activity as a Church, that it did not have any particular strategy for proclaiming the faith to the heathen, and that nevertheless this became the age of the greatest missionary success. The conversion of the ancient world to Christianity was not the result of any planned activity on the part of the Church but the fruit of the proof of the faith as it became visible in the life of Christians and of the community of the Church. The actual invitation from experience to experience—humanly speaking, the missionary strength of the early Church was nothing else. The Church's community of life invited people to share in this life in which was revealed the truth from which this kind of life arose. On the other hand the apostasy of the modern age rests on the disappearance of the verification of faith in the life of Christians. In this is to be seen the great responsibility of Christians today. They should be reference points of faith as people who know about God, should in their lives demonstrate faith as truth, and should thus become signposts for others.

The new evangelization we need so urgently today is not to be attained with cleverly thought out ideas, however cunningly these are elaborated: the catastrophic failure of modern catechesis is all too obvious. It is only the interaction of a truth conclusive in itself with its proof in the life of this truth that can enable that particular evidence of the faith to be illuminated that the human heart awaits: it is only through this door that the Holy Spirit enters the world.

I, Thou, and We in Faith

The mediation of faith through Jesus and its secondary mediation through the saints are linked together in a way that provides a third way of looking at the whole question. The act of faith is a profoundly personal act that is anchored in the inmost depths of the human ego. But precisely because it is so completely personal it is also an act of communication. In its profoundest nature the "I" always refers to the "thou" and vice versa: real relationship that becomes "communion" can only be born in the depths of the personality. The act of faith, we said, is a sharing in the vision of Jesus, propping oneself up on Jesus: John, who leant on Jesus' bosom, is a symbol for what faith means.[14] Faith is communion with Jesus and thus liberation from the repression that is opposed to the truth, liberation of my ego from its going against the grain of its being, so as to respond to the Father and say "yes" to love, "yes" to being, to say that "yes" that is our redemption and that overcomes the "world."

In this way faith by its inmost essential nature involves other people: it is a breaking out of the isolation of my ego that is its own illness.

The act of faith is an opening out into the distance, a breaking down of the door of my subjectivity, described by Paul in the phrase: "It is no longer I who live, but Christ who lives in me" (Gal. 2:20).[15] The redeemed ego finds itself again in a greater new ego. Paul describes this process of the dissolution of the first ego and its reawakening in a greater ego as being born again. In this ego into which I am liberated by faith I find myself united not only with Jesus but with everybody who has followed the same path. To put it another way, faith is necessarily what may be called churchly faith. It lives and moves in the "we" of the Church, one with the common "I" of Jesus Christ. In this new subject the wall between myself and others falls down: the wall that divides my subjectivity from objectivity and makes it unattainable for me, the wall between me and the depth of being. In this new subject I am contemporaneous with Jesus, and all the experiences of the Church are mine too, and have become my own.[16]

Of course this rebirth is not instantaneous but runs through the entire path of my life. But what is essential is that I cannot build my personal faith in a private dialogue with Jesus. Faith lives in this "we," or else it is not alive. Faith and life, truth and life, "I" and "we," are not divisible, and it is only in the context of sharing in the life of the "we" who believe, the "we" of the Church, that faith develops its logic, its organic shape.

Here admittedly the question can arise: "Where do I find the Church? Where, beyond its official teaching and its sacramental order, will I able to experience it as what it is?" This question can become one of genuine and urgent distress. And this despite the fact that today, alongside the parish as the normal sphere in which the Church is experienced, newly formed communities offer themselves, communities that have sprung directly out of the sharing of believers and give this the freshness of immediate experience. *Comunione e Liberazione* is this kind of place where the Church can be experienced and thus a place of access to fellowship with Jesus, to sharing in his vision. For such a movement to remain healthy and become truly fruitful it is important to hold two aspects in the correct balance. To begin with this kind of community must be really Catholic, that is, it must bear in itself the life and the faith of the universal Church of all places and all ages and let itself be shaped by this. If it does not sink its roots into these common foundations it becomes sectarian and futile. But on the other hand the universal Church becomes abstract and unreal if it is not presented here and now, in this place and in this time, in an actual community as a living thing. Thus it is the vocation of such movements to live out a true and profound catholicity in their individual communities, whatever form they may take, including the suppression of individual peculiarities that this means. Then they become fruitful and become themselves the Church, the place where faith is born and the place of rebirth into the truth.

· 2 ·

HOPE

The Optimism of the Modern Age
and Christian Hope

IN THE FIRST HALF of the 1970s one of our circle
undertook a journey to Holland, whose Church had
increasingly become a talking point—seen by some as an
image of hope of the better Church of tomorrow,
regarded by others as a symptom of the disintegration
that was the logical consequence of the attitude adopted.
With some curiosity we awaited the report our friend
gave us after his return home. Because he was an honest
man and an accurate observer, all the phenomena of the
disintegration were carefully mentioned: empty seminar-
ies, religious orders with no novices, priests and religious
who in shoals were turning their backs on their vocation,
the disappearance of confession, the dramatic decline in
Mass attendance, and so on. Of course the innovatory
experiments were mentioned too, even though they could
not change anything with regard to these symptoms of
decline but rather confirmed them. The real surprise
about this report came in the summing up it led up to:

despite everything a wonderful Church, since nowhere was there any pessimism, everyone was looking forward to the morrow with optimism. The phenomenon of general optimism allowed all the decadence and destruction to be forgotten: it sufficed to make up for all that was negative.

I thought to myself: what would one say of a businessman whose accounts were completely in the red but who, instead of recognizing this evil, finding out its reasons, and courageously taking steps against it, wanted to commend himself to his creditors solely through optimism? What should one's attitude be to an optimism that was quite simply opposed to reality? I tried to get to the bottom of the matter and looked at a number of hypotheses. Optimism could possibly be merely a cover behind which lurked the despair that one was trying to overcome in this way. It could be something worse: possibly this optimism was the method come up with by those who desired the destruction of the old Church and under the guise of reform wanted without much fuss to build a totally different Church, a Church after their own taste—something they could not set in motion if their intention was noticed too soon. In this case the public optimism would be a way of reassuring the faithful in order to create the climate in which one could dismantle the Church as quietly as possible and gain power over it. There would thus be two parts to the phenomenon of optimism: on the one hand it presupposed the trustfulness, indeed the blindness of the faithful who let themselves be reassured by fine words; on the other hand it consisted of a deliberate strategy to rebuild the Church so that in it no other, higher will—God's will—would disturb us any longer and prick the conscience but instead our own will would have the last word. It would thus ultimately be the optimism to liberate ourselves at last from the claim of the living God over our life, a claim that had become irksome for us. This optimism of the arrogance of apostasy would however make use of a naïve optimism on the other side and indeed deliberately nurture it, as if this kind of optimism were nothing other than the Christian's certainty of hope, the divine virtue of hope, whereas in reality it is a parody of faith and hope.

I considered yet another hypothesis: possibly this optimism that had been discovered was simply a variant of the liberal faith in continuous progress—the bourgeois substitute for the lost hope of faith. Finally I came to the conclusion that probably all these different components were at work together without it being easy to determine which of them had the decisive weight and when and where.

Somewhat later my work led me to occupy myself with the work of Ernst Bloch, for whom the "principle of hope" is the central figure in his thinking. According to Bloch hope is the ontology of what does not yet exist. The right kind of philosophy ought not to aim at investigating what is (that would be conservatism or reaction): it must rather—and this would be its true business—prepare what is not yet. What is has the value that it perishes: the world that is really worthy of life has yet to be built. The task of creative humanity would thus be to create this right kind of world that does not yet exist, and for this supreme task philosophy would have a decisive function to fulfill: it is the laboratory of hope, the anticipation in thought of the world of tomorrow—the anticipation of a rational and human world that would no longer be the result of accident but would be thought out and operated by us human beings and our reason. What surprised and struck me against the background of the experiences I have just recounted was the use of the word "optimism" in this context: for Bloch (and for many theologians who follow him) optimism is the shape and expression of belief in history and thus obligatory for someone who wishes to serve liberation, the revolutionary ushering in of the new world and the new man.[1] According to this, hope would be the virtue of an aggressive ontology, the dynamic force of the march towards utopia.

It dawned on me as the result of this reading that "optimism" is the theological virtue of a new god and a new religion, the virtue of deified history, of a god "history," and thus of the great god of modern ideologies and their promise. This promise is utopia, to be realized by means of the "revolution," which for its part represents a kind of mythical godhead, as it were a "God the son" in relation to the "God the father" of history. In the Christian system of virtues despair, that is to say, the radical antithesis of faith and hope, is labelled as the sin against the Holy Spirit because it excludes the latter's power to heal and to forgive and thereby rejects salvation.[2] Corresponding to this is the fact that in the new religion "pessimism" is the sin of all sins, for to doubt optimism, progress, utopia is a frontal attack on the spirit of the modern age: it is to dispute its fundamental creed on which its security rests, even though this is always under threat in view of the weakness of the sham god of history.

I was reminded of all this by the debate that was aroused in 1985 by the appearance of *The Ratzinger Report*. The indignation sparked by this modest little work culminated in the accusation that it was a pessimistic book. In many places efforts were made to stop its being sold, because a heresy of this magnitude simply could not be tolerated. The molders of public opinion placed it on the index of forbidden books: the new inquisition let its strength be felt. It showed once again that there is no worse sin against the spirit of the age than to show oneself lacking in optimism. It was not at all a question whether what was claimed was true or false, whether the diagnosis was correct or not: I have not been aware of people taking the time to investigate such old-fashioned

questions. The criterion was quite simple: "Is it opti-
mistic or not?"—and it completely failed this test. The
discussion that was aroused over the use of the term
"restoration," which did not really have anything to do
with what was actually said in the book itself, was only a
part of the debate: the dogma of progress seemed to be
called into question. With the rage that only sacrilege can
call forth people let fly at this denial of the god of history and its promises. I was struck by a parallel in the
field of theology. Many people link prophecy on the one
hand with criticism (revolution) and on the other with
optimism, and in this form make it the central criterion
for distinguishing between true and false theology.

Why am I saying all this? I think one can only understand the true nature of Christian hope and can only live
it afresh if one sees through for what they are its imitations and distortions that are trying to foist themselves
on to it. The greatness and the reasonableness of Christian hope come to light again only if we liberate ourselves
from the pinchbeck allure of their secular imitations.
Before we can take up the business of reflecting positively
on the nature of Christian hope it therefore seems to me
important to summarize and complete the findings we
have achieved so far. We said there was today an ideological optimism that could be described as the fundamental
act of faith of modern ideologies. This now needs to be
expanded under three heads:

(I) Ideological optimism, this surrogate for Christian hope, has to be distinguished from the kind of optimism that springs from someone's temperament and nature. This kind of optimism is simply a natural psychological disposition that can be linked equally with Christian hope or with ideological optimism but that does not coincide with either. Temperamental optimism is a fine thing and useful in life's hardships and suffering: who would not rejoice over the natural happiness and confidence that shines out from some people, and who would not want it for himself or herself? Like all natural tendencies, this kind of optimism is first of all a morally neutral quality; and again like all predispositions it must be developed and cultivated in order to play a positive role in shaping someone's moral physiognomy. Then by means of Christian hope it can grow and become yet purer and more profound: on the other hand it can collapse into an empty and misguided existence and become a mere façade. What remains important for our discussion is not to confuse it with ideological optimism but at the same time not to equate it with Christian hope, which as we have said can build on it but as a theological virtue is a human quality of much greater profundity and of a different class.

(2) Ideological optimism can exist both on a liberal and on a Marxist foundation. In the first case it is faith in progress through evolution and through the scientifically

guided development of human history. In the second case
it is faith in the dialectical movement of history, in
progress through the class struggle and revolution. The
contrasts between these two fundamental tendencies of
thought are obvious: both are again split up into different
variants of the basic pattern—"heresies" that spring from
the same trunk. But the differences that are visible, especially in the political field, should not deceive one about
the ultimate profound unity of the thinking that is at
work in them. Their kind of optimism is a secularization
of Christian hope: they depend ultimately on the transition from the transcendent God to the god "history." It
is here that is to be found the profound irrationalism of
these views, despite all their superficial rationality.

(3) Finally we must pay attention to the different ways
in which optimism and hope act in order to get the nature
of each in view. The goal of optimism is the utopia of the
finally and everlastingly liberated and fortunate world, the
perfect society in which history reaches its goal and
reveals its divinity. The immediate aim, which as it were
guarantees the reliability of the ultimate goal, is the success of our ability to do things. The goal of Christian
hope is the kingdom of God, that is the union of world
and man with God through an act of divine power and
love. The immediate aim that shows us the way and confirms the rightness of the ultimate goal is the perpetual
presence of this love and this power that accompanies us

in what we do and takes us up at the point where the potential of our own ability to act comes to an end. The internal justification for optimism is the logic of history, which goes its own way and presses forward irrevocably towards its goal: the justification of Christian hope is the incarnation of God's word and love in Jesus Christ.

If we now try to express what has been said in a more philosophical and theological terminology in something approaching the speech and thought of our everyday life, we can say that the goal of the ideologies is finally and ultimately success, in which we are able to realize our own wishes and plans. Our own ability and activity on which we are betting is however aware that ultimately it is guided and confirmed by an irrational fundamental tendency of development; the dynamic of progress means that everything ultimately becomes all right, as I was told recently by a physicist who regarded himself as important when I had the temerity to utter doubts about some modern techniques for handling nascent human life. The aim of Christian hope, by contrast, is a gift, the gift of love, which is given us beyond all our activity: to vouch for the fact that this thing that we cannot control or compel and that is yet the most important thing of all for human beings does exist, and that we are not clutching at thin air in waiting insatiably for it, we have the interventions of God's love in history, most powerfully in the figure of Jesus Christ in whom God's love encounters us in person.

But this means that the product of the promise of optimism is something that we must ultimately produce ourselves, trusting that the blind process of development in connection with our own activity will finally lead to the right goal. The gift of the promise of hope, on the other hand, is precisely that, a gift that as something already bestowed we await from him who alone can really give: the God who in the midst of history has already begun his age through Jesus. This in turn means that in the first case there is in reality nothing to hope for, because what we are awaiting we must bring about ourselves, and nothing will be given us beyond what we can achieve ourselves. But in the second case real hope does exist beyond all our potential and possibilities, hope in the unbounded love that at the same time is unbounded power.[3]

In reality ideological optimism is merely the façade of a world without hope that is trying to hide from its own despair with this deceptive sham. This is the only explanation for the immoderate and irrational anxiety, this traumatic and violent fear that breaks out when some setback or accident in technological or economic development casts doubt on the dogma of progress. The delight in horrors, the violent gestures of a mutually encouraged fear that we experienced after Chernobyl had something irrational and eerie about it, to the extent that it can only be understood if something much more profound lies behind it than an accident that, however serious, was nevertheless limited. The violence that marks these outbreaks of anxiety and fear is a kind of self-defense against the doubts that threaten belief in the ideal world of the future, since human beings are by their nature directed toward the future. We cannot live if this fundamental element of our being becomes void.

This is where the problem of death crops up. Ideological optimism is an attempt to have death forgotten by continually talking about history striding forward to the perfect society. The fact that this is to skirt round what is really important and that people are being soothed with a lie becomes obvious whenever death itself moves into the vicinity. The hope of faith, on the other hand, reveals to us the true future beyond death, and it is only in this way that the real instances of progress that do exist become a future for us, for me, for every individual.

Three Biblical Examples of the Nature of Christian Hope

To understand the nature of Christian hope from within let us now simply turn to the basic document, the Bible—though not in the sense of a systematic investigation of what it has to say about hope. Instead I would like to single out just three passages where the essential distinction between "optimism" and hope becomes quite clear and where through this method of contrast what is specific and distinctive about believing hope is clarified.

The Prophet Jeremiah

The classical example of the distinction we are talking about is provided for me by the prophet Jeremiah. Because of his pessimism he was condemned and imprisoned. The official optimism of the military, the nobility, the priesthood, and the establishment prophets demanded the conviction that God would protect his city and his temple. God was thus degraded to become the guarantee of human success and misused as the justification for irrationalism. The real, empirically comprehensible situation excluded a Jewish military success against the Babylonians. The rational outcome of a sober analysis of the situation had therefore to be to strive for an honorable compromise, as long as the enemy was prepared to concede this. The official optimism on the contrary demanded a continuation of the struggle and the firm conviction that this would end in victory. The contrast between Jeremiah on the one hand and Israel's religious and political élite on the other provides a valid representation of the nature of the contrast between on the one hand a theology that has become politicized, irrational, and directed at ideological power, and on the other the

realism of the believer who incorporates genuine morality and political rationality. In this realism the different
levels of human being and human thought are related to
each other correctly without confusion or false distinction.[4] From the point of view of official optimism the
prophet's realism appeared as gross and inadmissible pessimism.

Typical of this opposition is the encounter between
Jeremiah and Hananiah, the prophet of success who justified and defended the official optimism. Jeremiah, the
true prophet, depends by contrast on the realism of reason as a moral duty, condemns ideological optimism, and
lets God's promise and its in fact unconquerable hope
become visible (Jer. 28). The criterion that Jeremiah lays
down in v. 9 remains valid: the proclamation of empirical
successes is to be judged by empirical criteria and cannot
rely on theology. Anyone who today proclaims an ideal
and perfect society for tomorrow must provide empirical
proof for this announcement and cannot gloss over his or
her claim with theological arguments. The message of
God's kingdom and salvation cannot be adduced as proof
that certain social techniques will bring forth a society
that functions within history and does so empirically.

In Israel's catastrophic defeat, the collapse of all the
preceding varieties of optimism, Jeremiah the pessimist
showed himself to be the true bearer of hope. For the
others everything had necessarily to have come to an end

with this defeat: for him everything at this moment was beginning anew. God is never defeated, and his promises do not collapse in human defeats: indeed, they become greater, as love grows to the extent that the beloved has need of it. Israel's defeat and the official extinction of its national existence became the hour of the "pessimist" Jeremiah and his message of hope: in this moment the prophet finds immortal words of comfort. He provides the power to start again and to hope, which endured through the darkness of seventy years' exile up to the return home. It was precisely in this hour that the proclamation of the new covenant was born (Jer. 31:31–34), the new presence of God through his Spirit in our hearts. From this hour date words that at the last supper Jesus was to take up again and disclose in their full meaning (cf. Luke 22:20)—in the hour of his defeat by death, which was also his final and definitive victory.

For his rejection of official optimism Jeremiah was condemned as a pessimist. But this "pessimism" is inseparably one with the greater and unconquerable hope that he proclaimed: indeed, it was only this true hope that enabled him to display the realism of resistance to mendacious optimism. In this inseparable unity of realism and true hope Jeremiah is incidentally the representative of all true prophets. The theory put forward by many scholars that all great prophets have been prophets of doom is false. But it is correct that their genuinely theological hope did not coincide with superficial optimism and that, as bearers of true hope, these great figures were at the same time relentless critics of current parodies of hope.

The Revelation of St. John

A second example that will help elucidate our question is provided by the Apocalypse, or Revelation, of St. John. The vision of history that is displayed there represents the greatest possible antithesis one can imagine to faith in perpetual progress. To the extent that the course of history depends on human decisions it appears in this vision as a perpetual recurrence of the episode of the tower of Babel. Men and women are continually trying afresh to build bridges to heaven through their own technical ability, that is, by their own power to turn themselves into God. They are trying to give man that complete freedom, that absolute well-being, that unlimited power that seems to him to be the nature of the divine that one would like to bring down to one's own existence from the unattainable heights of the totally other. These efforts that sustain human behavior in all periods of history rest however on falsehood, on a "suppression of the truth": man is not God; he is a finite and limited being, and by no power of whatever kind can he make himself what he is not. For this reason all these attempts, however gigantic their beginnings may be, must end with collapse into destruction: their foundations will not hold.

But alongside this one historical factor—the Sisyphus-like efforts to bring heaven down to earth—the Apocalypse knows a second force in history: the hand of God. Superficially it appears as punitive, but God does not create evil and does not will the suffering of his creatures. He is not an envious God. In reality this hand of God is the force that gives hope to history despite and in opposition to the power of self-destructive behavior based on falsehood: the hand of God impedes man when it comes to the final implementation of self-destruction. God does not permit the annihilation of his creation. That is the meaning of his action at the building of the tower of Babel, the meaning of all his interventions described in the Apocalypse. What is represented there as divine punishment is not a scourge wielded in a positivistic sense from outside but the becoming visible of the internal legal status of a human action that is opposed to the truth and thus is directed toward nothing, toward death. The "hand of God" that is revealed in the inner resistance of being to its own destruction prevents the march into the abyss and thus bears the sheep that has gone astray back to the pasture of being, of love. Even when it is painful to be taken out of the thicket we have sought ourselves and to be brought back, it is nevertheless the act of our redemption, the event that gives us hope. And who could not see the hand of God even today grasping hold of man at the uttermost limit of his destructive rage and his perversions and preventing him from going further?

If we put everything together we can say that in the Apocalypse there is displayed the same mutual relationship between apparent "pessimism" and radical hope that we found in Jeremiah. The only thing is that what in the first case referred to a particular historical moment and its complex of situations is now extended to a comprehensive vision of history as a whole.[5] The Apocalypse is far removed from the promise of continual progress: still less does it recognize the possibility of establishing a once and for all fortunate and definitive form of society through our own human activity. Despite or rather precisely because of this rejection of irrational expectations it is a book of hope.

What it is ultimately telling us is this: despite all the horrors human history will not be drowned in the night of self-destruction; God will not let it be torn from his hands. The divine judgments, the great sufferings in which humankind is submerged are not instances of destruction but serve the salvation of humankind. Even "after Auschwitz," even after the most tragic catastrophe of history, God remains God: he remains good with an indestructible goodness. He remains the redeemer in whose hands man's destructive and cruel activity is transformed by his love. Man is not the only actor on the stage of history, and that is why death does not have the last word in it. The fact that there is this other person who is active is alone the firm and certain anchor of a hope that is stronger and more real than all the frightfulnesses of the world.

The Sermon on the Mount

My third example I take from the sermon on the mount, and essentially I would like to restrict myself to the beatitudes. In their linguistic and philosophical structure they are paradoxes. Let us take only one to demonstrate this quite graphically: "Blessed are those who mourn" (Matt. 5:4). To underline the paradox we could translate this as: "Blessed are those who are not overloaded with good fortune." The word "blessed" in the beatitudes has in this way nothing semantically to do with words like "happy" or "well." It is precisely this that the person who mourns is not. "Happy are those who are not happy" is how one would have to translate it to bring out the entire paradox.

But what strange kind of good fortune is it then that is meant by the word "blessed"? I think the word has two temporal dimensions: it embraces both present and future, and each in a different way. The present aspect consists of the fact that those addressed are told of a special closeness to them of God and his kingdom. This would then mean: It is precisely in the sphere of suffering and mourning that God with his kingdom is particularly close. When someone suffers and complains, God's heart is moved and affected in a special way. The complaint invokes his coming down to deliver this person (cf. Exod. 3:7). This presence of God's concern that is lurking in the word "blessed" includes a future: God's presence that is still hidden will one day be manifest. Hence what the phrase is saying is: Do not be afraid in your distress; God is close to you, and he will be your great comfort. The proportion of present and future varies in the different beatitudes, but the basic relationship is always the same.

In the paradoxes of the beatitudes we find reflected precisely the paradox of the figure of Jeremiah as well as the Apocalypse's portrait of history. The particular element of the beatitudes consists of the fact that the prophetic paradox now becomes the model of Christian life and existence. The beatitudes tell us: "If you live as Christians, you will always find yourselves in this paradoxical tension." What is meant becomes clear in the portrait of the apostle that Paul sketches in his second letter to the Corinthians. This picture seems to have developed precisely from the paradoxes of the sermon on the mount and illustrates it from what the apostle of the heathen experienced in his own life: "We are treated as impostors, and yet are true; as unknown, and yet well known; as dying, and behold we live; as punished, and yet not killed; as sorrowful, yet always rejoicing; as poor, yet making many rich; as having nothing, and yet possessing everything" (2 Cor. 6:8b–10).

A wonderful summary of this entire paradox of Christian existence, again shaped by the experience he has suffered and lived through, is to be found in 2 Cor. 4:16: "Though our outer nature is wasting away, our inner nature is being renewed every day." Our life's linear progression towards death is answered by the circle of divine love, which becomes a new line for us—the perpetual and progressive renewal of life in us, with life increasing simply according to the relationship that is established between me and the truth that has become a person, Jesus. The inescapable linearity of our path towards death is transformed by the directness of our path to Jesus: "Whether we live or whether we die, we are the Lord's" (Rom. 14:8).

Let us return to the beatitudes. In this matter we can now establish within the Bible a double line of movement. On the one hand the path leads from the figures of actual experience like Jeremiah and other prophets to the universally valid form expressed in the sermon on the mount, with the beatitudes breaking this one pattern down into a variety of forms. The beatitudes are not, as they are often misunderstood to be, a comprehensive ethical con-

spectus, a kind of New Testament decalogue, but a representation of the single Christian paradox realized in
different ways in keeping with the different fates men and
women encounter in their lives; in general they will not all
be found together to the same degree united in one person. On the other hand new patterns of actualization are
continually emerging from this general form, as we have
found in the case of the apostle Paul.

In order to grasp the true profundity of the beatitudes
and thereby the core of Christian hope, we must now
bring to light yet another aspect that, as far as I can see,
is little regarded in modern exegesis but that, I am convinced, is decisive for a faithful interpretation of the sermon on the mount as a whole: its inner logic depends on
the facts we are about to consider. What I have in mind
is the Christological dimension of this text.

To make it clear as quickly as possible what I am thinking of I shall start once again from an actual example—
a brief interpretation of the closing passage of Matthew's
version of the sermon on the mount (Matt. 7:24–27):

Every one then who hears these words of mine and
does them will be like a wise man who built his house
upon the rock; and the rain fell, and the floods came,
and the winds blew and beat upon that house, but it
did not fall, because it had been founded on the rock.
And every one who hears these words of mine and

does not do them will be like a foolish man who built his house upon the sand; and the rain fell, and the floods came, and the winds blew and beat against that house, and it fell; and great was the fall of it.

The immediately obvious meaning of the parable is a warning of Jesus to build one's own life on firm ground. The firm ground that stands fast in every storm is the word of Jesus himself. This immediate "moral" obviously has its own absolute worth. But the profundity as well as the promise of this passage becomes completely clear only if one pays attention to the hidden connection with another passage of Matthew: Matt. 16:13–20. Here too Jesus is speaking of a house that is to be constructed and that will be built on the rock so that it will not be destroyed by the powers of the abyss. The image and the language in both passages are the same down to the details, so that a connection is obvious. But in this second passage it is Jesus himself who builds the house: he behaves like the wise man who chooses a foundation of rock—he whom the same Gospel calls "wisdom" (Matt. 11:19). The old image of wisdom who built herself a house (Prov. 9:1–6) comes to mind.

Thus behind the moral significance the Christological level becomes visible, and it is this that gives the moral aspect the dimension of hope: if we remain alone with our own strength we do not succeed in building our life as a firmly established house. Our strength and our wisdom are not enough for that. Is human life therefore absurd, is it despair—a meaningless path towards death? The gospel tells us: there is the one who is truly wise; he has found the rock, and he himself (his word) is the rock; he himself has laid the foundation of the house. We are wise if we leave the foolish isolation of self-realization that builds on the sand of our own ability. We are wise if we do not try in isolation, with everyone acting for himself or herself, to build the purely private house of our own individual life. It is our wisdom to build the joint house with him so that we ourselves become his living house.

If it is right with Vatican II to read the Bible as a whole and as a unity, we should perhaps go yet one step further. In the Apocalypse we are told that the dragon—the great opponent of the redeemer—stood "on the sand of the sea" (Rev. 12:17).[6] Despite his great words, despite his immense and almost miraculous technical ability, despite his power and his crafty cunning, the monster does not know true wisdom but rounds off the image of the foolish man, just as Christ is the image of the wise man. And that is why the dragon ultimately disappears just as the house built on sand does: its fall was great. Once again in the contrast between Christ and the dragon we find the paradox of Christian hope, its empirical miserableness and its unconquerability: "Dying, and behold we live" (2 Cor. 6:9, cf. 4:7–12).

To return to the sermon on the mount: the closing parable with its hardly mistakable Christological background is for me a key that opens a door into the profundity of the text. The secret subject of the sermon on the mount is Jesus. It is only on the basis of this subject that we can discover the entire meaning of this key text of Christian faith and life. The sermon on the mount is not some exaggerated and unreal moral lecture that loses any definite relationship to our life and seems completely impractical. Nor is it, as the opposite hypothesis would have, merely a mirror in which it becomes clear that everyone is and remains a sinner in everything and can only reach salvation through unconditional grace. This contrast between moralism and the theory of pure grace, with a complete antithesis between law and gospel, does not help one to enter into the text but rather to repel it from one. Christ is the middle, the mean, that unites the two, and it is only discovering Christ in the text that opens it up for us and enables it to become a word of hope. This cannot be followed through in detail here: a hint will have to suffice. If we get to the bottom of the beatitudes, the secret subject Jesus appears everywhere. He it is in whom it becomes clear what it means to be "poor in spirit": it is he who mourns, who is meek, who hungers and thirsts for righteousness, who is the merciful. He is pure in heart, he is the peacemaker, he is persecuted for righteousness' sake. All the sayings of the sermon on the mount are flesh and blood in him.[7] In this way we can finally discern the text's twofold anthropological intention, its actual definite instructions for us:

(a) The sermon on the mount is a summons to follow Jesus Christ in discipleship. He alone is "perfect, as our heavenly Father is perfect" (the demand reaching into the depths of one's being in which the individual instructions of the sermon on the mount are condensed and united: Matt. 5:48). On our own we cannot "be perfect, as our heavenly Father is perfect"—but we must be to correspond to the task our nature lays upon us. We cannot do this, but we can follow him, cling to him, become his. If we belong to him as his limbs or members, then through our participation we become what he is: his goodness becomes ours. What the father says in the parable of the prodigal son is realized in us: "All that is mine is yours" (Luke 15:31). The moralism of the sermon on the mount that is all too stiff for us is brought together and transformed into communion with Jesus, into being a disciple of Jesus: in clinging fast to our relationship to him, in friendship with him and in confidence in him.

(b) The second aspect concerns the future hidden in the present. The sermon on the mount is a word of hope. In fellowship with Jesus what is impossible becomes possible: the camel goes through the eye of a needle (Mark 10:25). In being one with him we become capable too of

fellowship with God and thus of conclusive salvation. To
the extent that we belong to Jesus his qualities are realized
in us too—the beatitudes, the perfection of the Father.
The letter to the Hebrews explains this connection of
Christology and hope when it says we have a sure and
steadfast anchor of our life that enters into the inner
shrine behind the curtain, there where Jesus has entered
(Heb. 6:19–20). The new man is not utopian: he exists,
and to the extent that we are united with him hope is present and in no way merely future. Eternal life and the real
fellowship and community, liberation, are not utopia, the
mere expectation of what does not exist. "Eternal life" is
the real life, even today and at present in communion
with Jesus. Augustine emphasized this here-and-now
quality of Christian hope in his exposition of the saying
in Romans: "In this hope we were saved" (Rom. 8:24).
According to him Paul is teaching not that salvation will
be granted us but that we *are* saved. Of course we do not
yet see what we hope for. But we are already the body of
the head in whom everything is already present that we
are hoping for.[8]

Bonaventure and Thomas Aquinas on Christian Hope

Let me conclude this meditation on hope with two brief
considerations of the act of hoping, of the way in which

hope is to be lived out. In St. Bonaventure's Advent sermons I have found a wonderful parable of hope. The seraphic doctor told his hearers that the movement of hope was like the flight of a bird: in order to fly the bird stretches its wings out as far as possible and applies all its energies to the movement of flight; as it were it turns itself completely into movement and thus reaches the heights—and flies. To hope is to fly, said Bonaventure: hope demands of us a radical commitment; it asks of us that all our limbs become movement in order to lift off from the pull of the earth's gravity, in order to rise up to the true heights of our being, to God's promises. In this the Franciscan preacher developed a fine synthesis of the doctrine of the external and internal senses. Anyone who hopes, he said, "must lift up his head by directing his thoughts upwards, to the height of our existence, that is, to God. He must lift up his eyes in order to perceive all the dimensions of reality. He must lift up his heart by opening his feelings to the highest love and to all its reflections in the world. He must also move his hands in work. . . ."[9] So here too we find the essential element of a theology of work, which belongs to the movement of hope and when properly carried out is a dimension of it.

The supernatural, the great promise, does not push nature to one side. Quite the contrary: it calls forth the commitment of all our energies for the complete opening up of our being, for the unfolding of all its possibilities.

To put it another way, the great promise of faith does not destroy our activity, nor does it make it superfluous, but gives it for the first time its proper shape, its place and its freedom. A typical example of this is offered by the history of monasticism. It started with the *fuga saeculi*, the flight into the desert, the non-world, from a world that was shut in on itself. In this there prevailed the hope that precisely in this nothing as far as the world was concerned, in radical poverty, the everything of God, true freedom, would be found. But it was precisely this freedom of the new life that in the desert allowed the foundation of a new city, a new possibility of human life, a civilization of fraternity, out of which grew islands of life and survival in the collapse of the civilization of the ancient world.[10] "Seek first [the] kingdom [of God] and his righteousness, and all these things shall be yours as well," says our Lord (Matt. 6:33). History confirms what he says: it adds a quite human optimism to theological hope.

The second consideration follows a remark of St. Thomas Aquinas that was then taken up and developed in the Roman Catechism. In his *Summa Theologiae* Thomas says that prayer is the interpretation of hope.[11] Praying is the language of hope. The concluding formula of liturgical prayers, "through Christ our Lord," corresponds to the fact that Christ is realized hope, the anchor of our hoping. In his uncompleted compendium of theology Thomas intended to present the whole of theology in the pattern of faith, hope, and love. In fact the work ends with the first chapter of the second part and thus with the start of the section on hope. And this section in fact offers us an exposition of the Lord's Prayer. The Lord teaches us hope by teaching us his prayer, says Thomas. The Our Father is the school of hope—its actual practice.

In the Roman Catechism the exposition of the Our Father forms the fourth part of the basic Christian catechesis, alongside the explanation of the creed, of the commandments, and of the sacraments. Here too the Lord's Prayer functions as an exposition of hope. Those who despair do not pray any more because they no longer hope: those who are sure of themselves and their own power do not pray because they rely only on themselves. Those who pray hope in a goodness and in a power that transcend their own capabilities. Prayer is hope in execution.

If to start with we omit the first set of petitions in the Lord's Prayer, we can say that in the second set of petitions our daily cares and anxieties turn to hope. Here we find worry about how we shall make out on earth, peace with our neighbors, and finally the threat that outweighs all threats—the danger of losing the faith, of falling away from God into immeasurable distance from him, of no longer being able to perceive God and thus landing in absolute emptiness, exposed to each and every evil. By means of these worries becoming petitions the way is opened up from wishes and hopes to hope, from the second part of the Lord's Prayer to the first. All our anxieties are ultimately fear of losing love and of the total isolation that follows from this. Thus all our hopes are at bottom hope in the great and boundless love: they are hope in paradise, the kingdom of God, being with God and like God, sharing his nature (2 Pet. 1:4). All our hopes find their culmination in the one hope: thy kingdom come, thy will be done on earth as it is in heaven. The earth will become like heaven, it will itself become heaven. In his will is to be found all our hope. Learning to pray is learning to hope and thus learning to love.

HOPE AND LOVE

Hope and Love in the Mirror
of Their Antitheses

HOPE IS THE FRUIT of faith, we have said: in it our life stretches itself out towards the totality of all that is real, towards a boundless future that becomes accessible to us in faith. This fulfilled totality of being to which faith provides the key is a love without reserve—a love that is an immense affirmation of my existence and that discloses the fullness of all being to me in its breadth and depth. In it the creator of all things says to me: "All that is mine is yours" (Luke 15:31). God, however, is "all in all," "everything to everyone" (I Cor. 15:28): the person to whom he imparts all that is his is someone for whom there are no longer any ends or boundaries. The love that Christian hope approaches in the light of faith is not something purely private and individual: it does not enclose me in a little world of my own. This love opens up to me the whole of everything, which through love becomes "paradise." The worst anxiety of all, as we have already said, is the fear of not being loved, the loss of love: despair is thus the conviction that one has forfeited all love forever, the horror of complete isolation. Hope in the proper sense of the word is thus the reverse: the certainty that I shall receive that great love that is indestructible and that I am already loved with this love here and now.

Hope and love therefore belong immediately to each other, just as faith and hope are not to be separated from each other. Because in this way one can only understand love properly if it is seen from the perspective of hope (and of faith), I would like in this final section to linger a little longer with the subject of hope—naturally always with love in view, so that the true nature of love becomes visible in the mirror of hope. There is yet another point of view that needs to guide us in the steps we are about to take: the positive nature of something is often only revealed to us properly when we have grasped its opposites, its antitheses. In this way I would like to illuminate some of the barriers to hope that at the same time are also opponents of love.

Christian tradition is aware of two attitudes that are fundamentally opposed to hope: despair and presumption. Regardless of their apparent opposition, both attitudes are very close to each other and inwardly coincide. At first sight one might perhaps say that both are fringe manifestations of human existence that occur only in borderline cases and hence should not attract too much attention. If one defines the two concepts very strictly and narrowly that may perhaps apply—though, in the growing secularization of the world in which the human need for infinity runs up in vain against the towering wall of the finite, despair has long since ceased to be the exception and is continually becoming more frequent in the very age of hope in youth and even in childhood. Christian thought, however, has gone beyond this to work out an analysis of the entire system of acts and attitudes that all ultimately spring from the root of these two poisonous plants and thus bring to light their wide-ranging family. If one follows these analyses one discovers with astonishment how very precise a delineation they offer of the problems of our own age.

The Drying Up of Hope and Love in the Inertia of the Heart (*Accidie*)

Let us consider this tradition in the mirror of the thought of Thomas Aquinas, who took up the heritage of the ancient world and of the Fathers of the Church and provided a masterly synthesis.[1] According to him the root of despair is to be found in what has been termed accidie: for want of a better word we usually translate this as sloth or inertia, by which very much more, and something deeper, is meant than mere idleness, than lacking the inclination to be active. According to Thomas this meta-physical inertia is identical with the "sorrow of the world," the "worldly grief" of which Paul says that it produces death (2 Cor. 7:10). What is it about the mysterious sorrow of this world? Not that long ago this phrase would have seemed obscure if not unreal to us, since it seemed as if the children of this world were much more cheerful than the faithful, who seemed to be prevented from really enjoying life by being tormented by conscientious scruples and probably also glanced enviously across at the unbelievers who seemed to have the entire paradise of earthly delight standing open for them without reservations or anxieties. The great exodus from the Church was thought to be for precisely this reason, that at last people wanted to be free of the burdensome restrictions that meant that in fact not just one tree in the garden but virtually the whole lot seemed to be forbidden. . . . It seemed as if only unbelief could set one free to enjoy life. The yoke of Christ did not feel in any way "easy" or "light" for many Christians of the modern age: they experienced it as far too heavy, at least in the form in which they found it presented to them in the Church.[2]

Today, when the promises of unlimited freedom have been made the most of, we are beginning to understand afresh this saying about the "sorrow of the world." The forbidden joys lose their attraction the moment they are no longer forbidden. They had and have to be radicalized, the pitch increasingly raised, and nevertheless seem finally flat and stale because they are all finite while the hunger is for the infinite. Thus today we often see in the faces of young people a remarkable bitterness, a resignation that is far removed from the enthusiasm of youthful ventures into the unknown. The deepest root of this sorrow is the lack of any great hope and the unattainability of any great love: everything one can hope for is known, and all love becomes the disappointment of finiteness in a world whose monstrous surrogates are only a pitiful disguise for profound despair. And in this way the truth becomes ever more tangible that the sorrow of the world leads to death: it is only flirting with death, the ghastly business of playing with power and violence, that is still exciting enough to create an appearance of satisfaction. "If you eat it you must die"—for a long time this has no longer been just a saying from mythology (Gen. 3:3).

After this first attempt at the nature of the "sorrow of the world," otherwise known as metaphysical inertia, or accidie, let us have another and closer look at its physiognomy. On this the traditional Christian anthropology says that this kind of sorrow stems from a lack of greatness of soul (*magnanimitas*), from an incapability of believing in the greatness of the human vocation that has been destined for us by God. Man does not trust himself to his own true dimension but wants to be "more realistic." Metaphysical inertia would on this account be identical with that false humility that has become so common today: man does not want to believe that God is concerned about him, knows him, loves him, watches over him, is close to him.

Today there is a remarkable hatred among people for their own real greatness. Man sees himself as the enemy of life, of the balance of creation, as the great disturber of the peace of nature (which would be better off if he did not exist), as the creature that went wrong. His salvation and the salvation of the world would on this view consist of his disappearing, of his life and soul being taken back from him, of what is specifically human vanishing so that nature could return to its unconscious perfection in its own rhythm and with its own wisdom of dying and coming into being.

At the start of the road stood the pride of wanting to "be like God." We had to shake off the Big Brother God who is spying on us in order to be free, take back into ourselves the God projected into the heavens and ourselves rule over creation as God. Thus there arose in fact a kind of spirit and will that was and is opposed to life and is a dominion of death. The more perceptible this becomes the more the original intention turns into its opposite while remaining trapped in the same point of departure: man who only wanted to be his own creator and to reassemble creation himself with a better form of evolution he had thought out himself—this man ends in self-negation and self-destruction. He finds it would be better if he were not there.[3] This metaphysical inertia (*accidie*) can coexist with a great deal of activity and busy-ness. Its nature is the flight from God, the wish to be alone with oneself and one's finiteness and not to be disturbed by the presence of God.

In the history of Israel, as portrayed for us by Holy Scripture, we encounter such attempts very frequently: Israel finds the fact that it has been chosen, this having constantly to go with God, too demanding. People would sooner go back to Egypt, to normality, and be like all the others. This rebellion by human sloth and inertia against the greatness of being chosen is an image of the revolt against God that continually recurs throughout history and that characterizes our own epoch in a particular way. Man rebels not against this or that but in an attempt to shake off being chosen. If being loved by God makes too much of a claim on him, becomes a disturbance he does not want, then he revolts against his own nature. He does not want to be what he now is as this part of creation. In this context it strikes me that an essay Josef Pieper wrote in 1935, clearly with the spirit of Nazism in view, is very topical: anyone who reads it sees at once that it has gained new though altered relevance today. Pieper wrote then that "lethargic sorrow" was "one of the determining traits in the secret countenance of our age, the same age that has proclaimed the model of the 'world of total work.' This lethargy," he continued, "defines, as a symptom of secularization, the visage of any age in which the vocation to the real Christian tasks begins to lose the characteristic of public obligation. . . . It is not through 'working' that one annihilates despair (at least consciousness of it) but only through the clear-sighted greatness of spirit that the greatness of one's own existence expects and demands and through the blessed encouragement of hope in eternal life."[4]

What is important about this passage is not just the reference to the connection between external activity and ultimate refusal, profound existential inertia. Beyond this what seems to be important is that the greatness of soul of the human vocation reaches beyond the individual aspect of human existence and cannot be squashed back into the merely private sphere. A society that turns what is specifically human into something purely private and defines itself in terms of a complete secularity (which moreover inevitably becomes a pseudo-religion and a new all-embracing system that enslaves people)—this kind of society will of its nature be sorrowful, a place of despair: it rests on a diminution of human dignity. A society whose public order is consistently determined by agnosticism is not a society that has become free but a society that has despaired, marked by the sorrow of man who is fleeing from God and in contradiction with himself. A Church that did not have the courage to underline the public status of its image of man would no longer be the salt of the earth, the light of the world, the city set on a hill.

Even the Church can fall victim to metaphysical inertia, to accidie: an excess of external activity can be the pitiful attempt to cover up inward pusillanimity and slothfulness of the heart that springs from poverty of faith, from a lack of hope and of love for God and for man made in his image and likeness. Because one no longer dares to do the great things that are proper to one, one is forced all the more to live out of the past. But the feeling remains and continually grows that one is doing too little.

The Daughters of Inertia

The topicality of St. Thomas's analyses will become possibly even more obvious if we have a look at what he has to say about the "daughters of inertia." Along with despair what is born from the slothful retreat before the greatness of humanity loved by God is the *evagatio mentis,* the footloose restlessness of the mind, for, as Thomas says, "no man can dwell in sorrow."[5] But if the foundation of the soul is sorrow we are necessarily faced with a continual flight of the soul from itself, with a profound restlessness: man is afraid to be alone with himself, he loses his center and becomes a mental and spiritual vagabond who is always out. The symptoms of this footloose restlessness are garrulousness (*verbositas*) and inquisitiveness: from thought man runs away into talking; since he has lost the vision of eternity he is launched on an insatiable search for surrogates. Further attitudes reinforce this: inward restlessness (*importunitas—inquietudo*), that is to say, a persistent morbid search for the new as a substitute for the loss of the inexhaustible surprise of divine love; finally a physical restlessness and a changeability of will and purpose (*instabilitas loci vel propositi*).[6]

This analysis, though sketched only briefly, of the offspring of metaphysical inertia seems in many ways like a picture of the average psychological situation of today. But what is more important is that the diagnosis also shows the way to healing: only the courage to rediscover and accept the divine dimension of our being can give our souls and our society a new inner stability once again.

St. Thomas goes on to deal with four more daughters of accidie: apathy (*torpor*) with regard to everything man needs for salvation; faintheartedness (*pusillanimitas*); nursing grudges (*rancor*); and spitefulness (*malitia*). Only two of these need a brief comment. Rancor, the nursing of grudges, is today included by many as a component of the modern catalogue of virtue. But it is the opposite of that righteous indignation that the diminution of man according to the dimensions of positivism does not want to accept. It is man's fundamental discontentedness with himself that as it were takes its revenge on other people because they do not provide what could only be provided by a new opening up of one's own soul. Today it can often be observed in numerous variants even within the Church but it always stems ultimately from the fact that people do not want from the Church what it is its job to impart, the grace of being a child of God, and that they are then found to regard as inadequate everything else that the Church is offering, so that one disappointment follows another. The great expectation of Christian life remains that it should bestow the totally other, that which is nowhere to be found, the ideal community and with it the healing even of one's own inner self. But this expectation is transposed to the earthly and institutional aspect of the Church that is expected to be the ideal community, and as a result it can only end in unholy rage.

Related to this kind of attitude is the hatred of the apostate who has thrown the burden of the Christian vocation away and has given himself or herself an apparently simpler interpretation of being a Christian. Such people now defend this new interpretation both to themselves and to others as the true content of the Christian message, because no one can bear to have to regard himself or herself as an apostate. As a result, however, there arises an incurable hatred for everything that calls to mind the real greatness of this message. All this awakens the person's conscience and calls into question the self-justification in which such a person has taken refuge after the loss of faith. The downtrodden conscience speaks again from outside, and now everything that gives it voice must be crushed underfoot along with it. More generally we can say that the person who refuses his or her metaphysical greatness is an apostate with regard to the divine vocation of being human. The monstrous and enormous hatred that seethes in many terrorist organizations today cannot indeed be understood at all without this compulsion to crush one's conscience underfoot and along with it everything that recalls its message.[7]

Spitefulness (*malitia*) in the strict sense consists for Thomas Aquinas in deliberate rebellion against God, in hatred of God: a stance that is actually absurd and that becomes possible only when metaphysical inertia, the rejection of God's love, has become the core of someone's existence. Here it becomes clear that slothfulness or inertia (false humility) and pride of rejection are interlocked. Today we are discovering how this kind of outcome spreads and casts its spell over people who in the captivity of their rejection are driven to a hatred that can only be satisfied by the destruction of man. This kind of despair can also wear the mask of optimism. Indeed, the ideological optimism we have described earlier is fundamentally always a mask hiding despair.

Varieties of Self-Satisfaction: Bourgeois Pelagianism and the Pelagianism of the Pious

In order not to draw this meditation out too long I will skip an analysis of presumption, that twin-sister of despair: the common foundation of both attitudes lies in the error of thinking that one does not need God for the realization and fulfillment of one's own being. Following Josef Pieper closely, I would like merely to try to offer a few comments on two widespread forms in which this vice finds expression and which from a purely superficial point of view can appear harmless.[8]

The first variation of presumption that we need to talk about is the bourgeois liberal Pelagianism that rests on considerations such as these: "If God really does exist and if he does in fact bother about people he cannot be so fearfully demanding as is described by the faith of the Church. Moreover I'm no worse than the others: I do my duty, and the minor human weaknesses cannot really be as dangerous as all that." In this widespread attitude to life we find the human self-belittlement that we have already described in the case of accidie and the self-sufficiency with regard to infinite love that people think they do not need in their bourgeois self-satisfaction. Perhaps in times of peace one can live for quite a long time in this frame of mind. But at the moment of crisis people will either be converted from it or fall victim to despair.

The other face of this same vice is the Pelagianism of the pious. They do not want any forgiveness from God, nor indeed any gift at all from him. They want to be okay themselves, wanting not forgiveness but their just reward. They want security, not hope. By means of a tough and rigorous system of religious practices, by means of prayers and actions, they want to create for themselves a right to blessedness. What they lack is the humility essential to any love—the humility to be able to receive what we are given over and above what we have deserved and achieved. The denial of hope in favor of security that we are faced with here rests on the inability to bear the tension of waiting for what is to come and to abandon oneself to God's goodness. This kind of Pelagianism is thus an apostasy from love and from hope but also at the profoundest level from faith too. Man hardens his heart against himself, against others and ultimately against God: man needs God's divinity but no longer his love. He puts himself in the right, and a God that does not cooperate becomes his enemy. The Pharisees of the New Testament are an eternally valid representation of this deformation of religion. The core of this Pelagianism is a religion without love that in this way degenerates into a sad and miserable caricature of religion.

Fear, Hope, Love

If we talk of the connection between hope and love the subject of fear must finally also be touched on. The Pelagianism of the pious is a child of fear, of a damaged hope that cannot endure the tension of awaiting the uncompellable gift of love. So from hope arises anxiety, and that in its turn gives birth to the striving for security in which no uncertainty can remain. Love does not now overcome fear because the egoistic person does not want to entrust himself or herself to its kind of certainty that can always only be a certainty of dialogue. From this point of view fear must be exorcized independently of the others through what is at my own disposal—through what I do myself, through my own work.

This kind of striving for security rests on the total self-assertion of the ego, which refuses to take the risk of emerging from its shell and entrusting itself to the other. This is in fact the test for the absence of true love. On the other hand we need to cling firmly to a kind of fear that is not only compatible with love but necessarily follows from it: the fear of hurting the beloved, of destroying the foundations of love by one's own fault. Liberalism and the Enlightenment want to talk us into accepting a world without fear: they promise the complete elimination of every kind of fear. They would like to get rid of every "not yet," every reliance on other people and their inner tension, even though this is something that belongs essentially to hope and love. Anyone who liberates man from fear in this way liberates him from hope and love too.

"The fear of the Lord is the beginning of wisdom," says Scripture (Ps. 111:10), and this saying remains true even today. Being able to sin belongs to our fundamental situation as creatures ever since the Fall, and this danger we are in is as it were the ontological ground of proper and properly ordered fear. A Christian upbringing cannot aim at ridding man of every kind of fear: it would then be in contradiction to what we are. Its task must be to purify fear, to put it in its proper place, and to integrate it with hope and love so that it can watch over and aid these. Thus it is possible for the right kind of courage to grow, courage that man would not need if there were not reason to fear. But when people pretend to eliminate fear completely without remainder they are denying the threats directed against our salvation and the integrity of our being: fear that is repressed in this way and no longer has its proper place turns up again in the many disguises of a fundamental anxiety.

In our age, which has removed anxiety about salvation and sin from man and has thus apparently made him free from fear, these new anxieties are rampant and often take on the form of collective psychoses: fear of the scourge of the major illnesses that destroy people; anxiety about the consequences of our technological power; anxiety about the emptiness and meaninglessness of existence. Anyone who thinks of the overexcited reactions that followed Chernobyl sees how unmastered fear at the root of the human heart can at any time force itself to the surface in irrational explosions. All these anxieties are masks for fear of death, alarm at the finiteness of our being. This kind of fear and alarm appears once one encounters the infinite with anxiety instead of with love and thinks one has shaken this anxiety off by denying it. But fear of the finite is more alarming and hopeless than the rejected fear of the infinite could ever be, a fear in which the mystery of consolation always remains hidden to await us.

Anyone who loves God knows that there is only *one* real threat for man, the danger of losing God. For that reason we pray: "Lead us not into temptation, but deliver us from evil"—that is, from the loss of faith, from sin in general. Anyone who abandons God in order to be free from this true fear comes under a tyranny of fear without hope. The Gospel according to St. John tells us that our Lord presented the "fear of the Jews" as the fundamental obstacle to faith. In order to explain the opposition between faith and fear the evangelist particularly likes making use of the ambiguity of the Greek word δόξα (*doxa*), which to begin with means quite generally something like "appearance," "splendor," etc. This basic meaning now splits in two opposite directions. In one of them the word is used to denote mere appearance, what only "appears" to be but is not: in this way it also means opinion, the appearance of truth that it gives rise to. But on the other hand the word is also used for the real "splendor," for the glory of God, for the opinion he has of man and of the world; and this opinion is the truth, is reality.

These two kinds of "appearance" come into conflict in the world. Man's opinion is power. Even when it is not in agreement with the truth it exercises its power: one has to deal with it. Individuals also build up an image of themselves, an "appearance," through which they want to assert themselves in the opinion of others. They want to safeguard their "appearance" and thus are forced to bow to the appearance of others. Truth itself is far distant and does not show its power; but the opinion of men and women is there and is dominant. So one follows it. Man fears the close-at-hand appearance of the power of human opinion more than the distant and powerless light of truth. So people bow to the power of opinion and become its allies, its bearers. They become the slaves of appearance. Once they have begun to become involved with it they must go on following it step by step. They can indeed no longer break free of the net of shared pretense. In their actions they are guided no longer by reality but by how the others can be expected to react.

Opinion, untruth gains domination. The entire life of a society, political as well as personal decisions, can in this way rest on a dictatorship of untruth: of how things are presented and reported instead of reality itself. An entire society can thus fall from the truth into shared deceit, into a slavery of untruth, of not-being. The salvation offered by the Logos, by the word of God made man, is of its nature a liberation from the slavery of appearance, a return to the truth. But the transition from appearance to the light of truth takes place in the figure of the cross.

Today in the society shaped by the mass media this image of man and his world has obtained an oppressive new reality. What is shown and "appears" (on television, for example) is stronger than reality. The "appearance" of the world in the media is becoming more and more the real governance of the world. Fear of what appears becomes a universal power and damages the courage of the truth. Perhaps it is difficult for us to apply to our lives in practical terms the saying of Scripture that the fear of the Lord is the beginning of wisdom. But if we turn this saying around its practical content quickly shows up: the lack of the fear of God is the beginning of all folly. When the fear of God that has its proper place at the heart of the love of God no longer holds sway, people lose their standard, their criterion: fear of man exerts its domination over them, there emerges an idolatry of what appears, and thus the door is wide open for every kind of folly.[9]

The Essential Nature of Love

Up till this point the question of what love is may not have been broached, but nevertheless it has provided the underlying thread of our reflections. Now however we must at last tackle it directly. What then is "love"? And what is the relationship between "natural" and "supernatural" love? The first thing needed here is to ward off a tendency that would separate eros and religious love as if they were two quite distinct realities. But this is to distort both of them, because something wanting to be a purely "supernatural" love becomes powerless, while on the other hand to enclose love in the finite, to profane it and separate it from its dynamic reaching out to the eternal is to falsify even earthly love, which of its nature is a thirsting after infinite fullness.

Anyone who narrows love down to this world alone takes away its most profound identity: to it belongs a future without frontiers, an acceptance whose totality does not suffer being squeezed into the finiteness of space and time. The general principle that grace presupposes nature applies here too and precisely here. Hence on the other hand the attempt to live the new love that is a gift from God—*agape, caritas*—while ignoring or going against nature would necessarily degenerate into a caricature of this love. The creator and the redeemer is one and the same God. In redemption he does not take creation back but rather makes it whole and raises it up.[10] Even if the aim of our meditation is essentially to learn *agape,* we must for this reason first start with the attempt to understand what love is in general.

Love as Affirmation and Assent

In English the word "love" is today exposed to the danger of being downgraded to banality in a way that slowly seems to make its use impossible. Nevertheless we cannot renounce the primary words like "God," "love," "life," "truth," and so on, and we should not simply let them be snatched away from us. But it is precisely when we use the word in the fullness of its original meaning that the question becomes almost unanswerable of what exactly it denotes. The phenomenon it is trying to capture is too rich and has too many layers. Regardless of the multiplicity of its different aspects and levels we can say meanwhile that it denotes an act of fundamental assent to another, a "yes" to the person towards whom the love is directed: "it is good that you exist," is Josef Pieper's striking definition of the nature of love.[11] The lover discovers the goodness of being in this person, is happy because of his or her existence, says "yes" to this existence and confirms it. Even before any thought of self, before any desire or wish, there stands the simple business of being happy at the existence of the beloved, the "yes" to this "you." It is only in a second moment (not of time but of fact) that the lover discovers that in this way, because *your* existence is good, my own existence too has become better, more precious, happier. By saying "yes" to another, to "you," I receive myself made new and can now in a new way say "yes" to myself thanks to you.

Let us now consider a little closer the first step of this process, saying "yes" to "you," the affirmation of your existence, of your being there (and with this of existing in love and being based on love). This "yes" is a creative act, a new creation. In order to be able to live human beings need this affirmation. Biological birth is not enough: man can only accept his personality, his "I," in the power of the approval of his being that comes from another, from "you." This "yes" of the one who loves him (or of course her) imparts his existence to him in a new and definite way. In this he receives a kind of rebirth without which his actual birth would remain incomplete and leave him in conflict with himself. In order to find the validity of this statement confirmed one needs only think of the lives of people who have been abandoned by their parents in the first months of their existence and have not been taken up by a love that affirms and embraces their lives. It is only rebirth in being loved that completes birth and opens up for men and women the space of meaningful existence.

This insight can help us to understand something of the mystery of creation as of redemption. Here it becomes comprehensible that love is creative and that God's love was the force that created being out of nothing, the real foundation on which all reality stands. But on this basis we can also understand a little better that God's second "yes" that was made manifest on the cross is our rebirth and that it is only this rebirth that finally and definitively makes us alive. And lastly the awareness can dawn that as people who have been affirmed by God in this way we are called to share in his "yes." We have been asked to continue his creation, to be co-creators, by giving being to the other in a new way in the affirmation of love—letting the gift of love now really become a gift.

Love and Truth—Love and the Cross

If we look a little more closely at this affirmation that is the essential nature of love, further important aspects are revealed to us. We said that the lover affirms and confirms the being of the beloved and added in brackets that this being of the beloved indirectly includes being in general. If we now pursue this line of thought further two facts appear. In the first place it becomes clear that every love bears within itself a universal tendency. The world to which this beloved belongs seems different once I start to

love. The lover would as it were like to embrace the whole
world in and with his beloved. The encounter with the
one person restores the whole to me afresh. Of course,
love is a choice: it is directed not at millions but at precisely this person. But precisely in this choice, in this one
person, reality as a whole appears in a new light to me.
Pure universalism, general philanthropy (as in Schiller's
invocation *Seid umschlungen, Millionen,* "be embraced, ye millions," in the last movement of Beethoven's Ninth)
remains empty, while the quite definite and decisive
choice that falls on this one person gives the world and
other people back to me afresh and me to them.

   This observation is important because from this starting point we can also start to comprehend why God's universalism (God wants everyone to be saved) makes use of
the particularism of the history of salvation (from Abraham to the Church). Concern for the salvation of others
should not lead to this particularism being as good as
completely deleted: the history of salvation and the history of the world should not be declared to be simply
identical because God's concern must be directed at
everyone.[12] This kind of direct universalism would however destroy the true totality of God's activity that reaches
the whole precisely through selection and election.

   From these observations the way now leads to the second fact that we would now like to address. Affirmation
of this person would ultimately lose its meaning if being

as a whole were not good. The originally limited affirmation of love presupposes the general goodness of being. To put it another way, the "yes" of my love—it is good that you are—presupposes truth; it presupposes that the being of this man or woman is really good. Included in it is the idea that being of the other stems from a true good, from a true affirmation. Love needs truth. In this sense we can say that without a creator God who vouches for the goodness of what exists, love would lose its justification and become groundless.[13]

Here let us leave on one side the theological and ontological considerations that crop up in this context in order instead to consider a quite practical conclusion. The lover says an unconditional "yes" to the beloved. The one loves the other not because of this or that quality: instead he or she loves the person herself or himself, and though the person is revealed in his or her qualities, that person is more than the sum of them. Love relates to the person as the person is, with all his or her weaknesses. But real love, in contrast to the brief enchantment of a moment, has to do with truth and thus directs itself to the truth of the person, which can also be undeveloped or concealed or distorted. Of course, loves includes a creative readiness for forgiveness, but forgiveness presupposes the recognition of sin as sin. Forgiveness is healing, whereas approval of evil would be destruction, accepting the sickness and thus not being good for the other.

This becomes immediately understandable if we consider the example of a drug addict who has become the prisoner of his (or it could be her) vice. The person who really loves him does not follow the twisted will of this sick man, his desire to poison himself, but works for his true happiness: he or she will do everything possible to heal the beloved from his addiction, even painfully and even against the blinkered will of the addict. Another example: in a totalitarian system someone has saved his skin and possibly also his position but at the price of betraying a friend and betraying his own convictions, his soul. True love is ready to understand but not to approve, not to declare innocuous what is neither to be approved nor innocuous. Forgiveness has its inner way: forgiveness is healing, that is to say, it demands the return to the truth. Where it does not do that it becomes approval of self-destruction, puts itself in conflict with truth and thus with love too.[14]

From this one can understand what the "wrath of God" and the anger of the Lord are all about: necessary expressions of his love that is always identical with the truth. A Jesus who is in agreement with everybody and anybody, a Jesus without his holy wrath, without the toughness of the truth and of true love, is not the true Jesus as Scripture shows him but a miserable caricature. A presentation of the "gospel" in which the seriousness of God's wrath no longer exists has nothing to do with the biblical gospel. True forgiveness is something quite other than weakly letting things be. Forgiveness is exacting and makes demands on both the person who forgives and the person who receives forgiveness in that person's whole being. A Jesus who approves of everything is a Jesus without the cross, because the tribulation of the cross would not then be needed to bring men and women salvation. In fact to a noticeable extent the cross is being interpreted out of theology and its meaning changed so as to become merely an unpleasant accident or a purely political affair.

The cross as atonement, the cross as a way of forgiving and redeeming, does not fit into a certain modern pattern of thought. It is only when the connection of truth and love is seen properly that the cross becomes understandable in its true theological depth. Forgiveness has to do with truth, and for that reason it requires the cross of the Son and it requires our conversion. Forgiveness is indeed the restoration of truth, the renewal of being, and the overcoming of the lie that lurks in every sin: of its nature sin is always a departure from the truth of one's own being and thus from the truth of the creator, God.

We could also say that forgiveness is participation in the pain of transition from the drug of sin to the truth of love. It is preceding and accompanying someone on this path of death and rebirth. Only preceding and accompanying addicts in this way (for sin is always a "drug," the lie of false happiness) can enable them to let themselves be led through the dark journey of suffering. It is only by going ahead to enter into the suffering and into the death involved in the way of transformation that makes this journey bearable, because it is only in this way that in the dark night of the narrow way the light of hope in new life becomes visible. The reverse is true: only love gives the power to forgive, that is, to accompany the other on the road of the suffering that transforms. It is only this that makes it possible to accept and to endure with and on behalf of the other the death of the lie. It is only this that enables one to remain a bearer of the light in the pitch-black and seemingly endless tunnel and to make noticeable the fresh air of the promise that leads to rebirth.

From this has to be developed the theology of the cross that is a theology of the truth and of love: the cross of Christ means that he precedes us and that he accompanies us on the painful way of our healing and salvation. From here too the theology of baptism and penance is to be developed. The three subjects of the cross, baptism, and repentance belong together and are ultimately only the development of the single basic subject of the love that created the world and redeems it.

The fact that all this has very down-to-earth pastoral consequences does not really need to be said anymore. A pastoral practice of appeasement, of "understanding everything and forgiving everything" (in the superficial sense of this phrase) stands in glaring contrast to the biblical evidence. The correct pastoral practice leads to the truth, arouses love for the truth, and helps people to accept the pain of the truth. It must itself be a form of accompanying people on the difficult but beautiful way to new life that is also the way to true and lasting joy.

What Is Self-Love?

In our analysis of the nature of love the question of the ego has so far only cropped up in a secondary role. Now however we must tackle it directly. Is there really such a thing as "self-love"? Is this a meaningful concept and, if so, how must it be conceived? If we turn to the Bible for help with this question, we start off by running up against apparently contradictory stances. First of all there are sayings like this: "For whoever would save his life (his soul) will lose it; and whoever loses his life (his soul) for my sake and the gospel's will save it" (Mark 8:35). Another saying of Jesus' is even fiercer: "If anyone comes to me and does not hate his own father and mother and wife and children and brothers and sisters, yes, and even his own life"—again the Greek word is literally "soul"—"he cannot be my disciple" (Luke 14:26). On the same lines are the phrase about self-denial as a necessary condition for discipleship (Mark 8:34) and other passages. On the other hand we are told we must love our neighbor "as yourself." But this means that self-love, the affirmation of one's own being, provides the form and measure for love of one's neighbor too. According to this self-love remains a natural and necessary thing without which love of neighbor would lose its foundation.

How can one discover the inner unity between these two groups of texts? We do not want here to conduct any learned exegetical investigations: it should be enough to indicate a fundamental fact of biblical thinking in order to clarify this question. Man—every man and woman— is called to salvation. He is willed and loved by God, and his highest task is to respond to this love. He must not hate what God loves. He must not destroy what is destined for eternity. To be called to the love of God is to have a vocation for happiness. To become happy is a "duty" that is just as human and natural as it is supernatural. When Jesus talks of self-denial, of losing one's own life and so on, he is showing the way of proper self-affirmation ("self-love"), something that always demands opening oneself, transcending oneself. But this necessity of going beyond oneself, of leaving oneself behind, does not exclude genuine self-affirmation. Quite the contrary: it is the way of finding oneself and "loving" oneself. When forty years ago I read for the first time Bernanos's *Diary of a Country Priest* the last words of this suffering

soul made an indelible impression on me: it is not difficult to hate oneself; the grace of all graces would however
be to love oneself as a member of the body of Christ. . . .

The realism of this statement is obvious. There are
many people who live in conflict with themselves. This
aversion to oneself, this inability to accept oneself and to
be reconciled with oneself, is far removed from that self-
denial that the Lord wants. Those who cannot stand
themselves cannot love their neighbor. They cannot
accept themselves "as themselves" because they are
against themselves and are bitter as a result and the very
foundation of their life makes them incapable of loving.[15]

This however means that egoism and real self-love are
not only not identical but exclude each other. Someone
can be a great egoist and nevertheless be dissatisfied with
himself. Indeed, egoism is often precisely a consequence
of being torn apart oneself, of the attempt to create
another ego for oneself, whereas the right relationship to
the ego in freedom grows of itself. One could almost talk
of an anthropological circle: to the extent that people are
always seeking themselves, would like to bring about their
own self-realization, and are intent on the success and
fulfillment of their ego, this ego becomes objectionable,
annoying, and unsatisfactory. It dissolves itself into a
thousand forms, and in the end all that remains is the
flight from oneself, the inability to stand oneself, the
recourse to drugs or to the myriad other forms of self-

contradictory egoism. Only the "yes" that is given me by someone else makes me capable for my part of addressing this "yes" to myself, in and with the other. The "I" is realized by the "you." On the other hand it is true that only someone who has accepted himself can address a real "yes" to someone else. Accepting oneself, "loving" oneself, once again presupposes truth and demands a continual pilgrimage towards the truth.

In addition, as in the case of hope, a defective form of asceticism can destroy the foundations of proper Christian life in this case too. In recent history we find two such defective attitudes above all. First of all there is a false form of awareness that, in a continual rummaging through one's own conscience, a perpetual search for one's own perfection, directs all attention on to one's own ego, one's sins and virtues. It reaches the point of a religious egoism that prevents those concerned from simply opening themselves to the sight of God and looking at that from themselves. Obstinately pious people who are totally concerned with themselves have no longer any time to seek the face of God and to hear God's liberating and redeeming "yes." The opposite and nevertheless closely related danger is an exaggerated selflessness, a denial of oneself that becomes a repudiation of oneself, that no longer wants to accept the ego and thus lets it become the dominant power once again in a subtle form of egoism. A wrecked and oppressed ego cannot love.

Here too there applies the dictum that grace does not abolish nature but presupposes it. In this we could well recall what St. Paul said: it is not first the supernatural (τὸ πνευματικόν) but the other way round, first the natural (τὸ ψυχικόν) and then the supernatural (I Cor. 15:46). Supernatural love cannot grow if its human foundations are lacking. Divine love is not the negation or the destruction of human love but its deepening and radicalization in a new dimension.

The Nature and Way of *Agape*

Like every love, "supernatural" love comes from a "yes" that has been given to me but in this case from a greater "you" than any human being. It is the irruption of God's "yes" into my life through Jesus Christ's "yes" to us who had distanced ourselves from God's "yes," a "yes" upheld in the incarnation, the cross, and the resurrection. *Agape* thus presupposes that the crucified love of the Lord has become perceptible to me, that it touches me through faith. From the point of view of human psychology that seems difficult: the well-known problem of making it present and actual stands in the way. How can the cross of the Lord come through to me from history so that I am able to experience the living reality that Pascal perceived in his meditation on the Lord on the Mount of

Olives: "I shed those drops of blood for you?"[16] Making it all present and actual is possible because the Lord lives even today in his saints and because in the love that comes from their faith his love can touch me directly. Let us recall here what we said in the section on faith about our path from a faith at second hand to a faith at first hand: in all encounters with the love of the saints, with those who really believe and love, I always encounter more than these particular men and women. I encounter the new thing that can only become of them through the other, through him, and thus the way is opened up in me too for direct access to him.

But this is only the first step. If this "yes" of the Lord really penetrates me so that it makes my soul reborn, then my own ego is saturated with him, is marked by sharing in him: "It is no longer I who live, but Christ who lives in me" (Gal. 2:20). Then what applies is the mystery of the body of Christ, as John Eudes has expounded it in his essay on the heart of Jesus: "Remember that our Lord Jesus Christ is your true head and that you are one of his members. He is to you as the head is to the members of the body; all that is his is yours. His spirit, his heart, his body, his soul, all his faculties, all are to be used by you as if they were yours. . . . For your part, you are to him as a member to the head, and he earnestly desires to use all your faculties as if they were his own. . . ."[17] In the encounter with Christ there occurs, to use the technical language of theology, a *communicatio idiomatum,* a mutual inward exchange in the great new "I" into which I am led and made at home by the transformation of faith. So then the other is no longer a stranger at all for me: he is part of me. Christ wishes to use my faculties and capabilities for him, even when a purely human natural attraction does not exist. Now I can give him Christ's "yes" that fills my life as my own "yes" and yet his, even when and precisely when natural sympathy is not there. In the place of individual, private sympathies and antipathies there has entered Christ's sympathy, his compassion, his suffering with and loving with people. From this compassion of Christ that has been communicated to me and that becomes my own in the life of faith I can hand on a compassion, a "yes," that is greater than my own and that enables the other to feel that profoundest "yes" that alone gives meaning and support to every human "yes."

It is no longer possible here to consider the human process of such *agape.* It demands practice, patience, and also the acceptance of continual setbacks. It presupposes that in the life of faith I come to the inward exchange of my ego with Christ so that his "yes" really penetrates into my being and becomes mine. It also presupposes practice on the part of the other: actually to venture this "yes" from him to the other for whom I am needed. It is only in this kind of risk-taking, at first still unaccustomed and perhaps a little frightening, that the power to do so grows and the Easter connection becomes ever more recognizable: this crucifixion of oneself—self-denial—leads to a great inner joy, to "resurrection." The more I dare lose myself, the more I discover that it is precisely in this way that I find myself. Thus through the encounter with Jesus a new realism accrues to me, and he again strengthens me anew in acting from membership with him. Just as there is such a thing as a vicious circle, a state of being imprisoned in the negative when one "no" leads to another and makes the whole thing ever more impossible to get out of, so there is also what could be called a healing circle, a circle of salvation, in which one "yes" gives birth to another. It is important that in this the right relationship of nature and grace should always be safeguarded. An *agape* that is not sustained and affirmed by my own nature, that aims at pushing the self to one side and challenging it, becomes sullen and obstinate. It frightens the other person off and nourishes the internal conflict within myself.

The challenge of the cross is something quite different. It reaches deeper: it demands that I give my ego into Jesus' hands, not so that he may destroy it but so that in him it may become free and expand. The "yes" of Jesus Christ that I hand on is only really his if it has also become completely mine. Thus a great deal of patience and humility also belongs to this way, just as the Lord has patience with us: it is not a headlong leap into heroism that makes someone a saint but patiently and humbly walking with Jesus, step by step. Holiness does not consist in adventurous achievements of virtue, but in joining him in loving. Hence the real saints are also the quite human, quite natural people in whom through the Easter transformation and purification what is human appears afresh in its total originality and beauty.

A Saying from the Sermon on the Mount

I would like to conclude these considerations with a few thoughts about three verses from the sermon on the mount that seem unreal, indeed scandalous, if one reads them in the perspective of a purely human morality, whereas they open themselves up to a Christological examination such as we have fundamentally been considering in the preceding meditations.

I am thinking of Matthew 5:38–39 and 41: "You have heard that it was said, 'An eye for an eye and a tooth for a tooth.' But I say to you, do not resist one who is evil. But if any one strikes you on the right cheek, turn to him the other also." To understand this text properly we must first recall that the Old Testament principle "eye for eye, tooth for tooth" (Exod. 21:24, Lev. 24:20, Deut. 19:21) is in no way the canonization of vindictiveness but quite the contrary, an attempt to replace the principle of revenge

by the principle of law. The basic principle of the sons of
Cain was (and is): "If Cain is avenged sevenfold, truly
Lamech seventy-sevenfold" (Gen. 4:24). In contrast to
this the principle of correspondence is being established
here: crime and punishment must balance. The law must
be upheld, but its implementation must not degenerate
into revenge.

Jesus did not in any way reject the principle of equal-
ity as a basic legal principle but rather wanted here to
open up to man a new dimension of his behavior. Law in
isolation and made absolute becomes a vicious circle, a
cycle of retaliation from which finally there is no way out
any longer. In his relationship with us God has broken
through this circle. In the face of God we are in the
wrong, having turned away from him in the search for our
own glorification and thus fallen victim to death. But
God renounces the punishment that would be just and
replaces it by something new: salvation, our conversion to
a renewed "yes" to the truth of ourselves. For this transformation to occur he goes ahead of us and takes the pain
and suffering of transformation upon himself. The cross
of Christ is the real discharging of this saying: not eye for
eye, tooth for tooth, but the transformation of evil
through the power of love. In his whole human existence,
from the incarnation to the cross, Jesus does and is what
is said here. He bursts our "no" open by means of a
stronger and greater "yes." In the cross of Christ and only

there this saying opens up and becomes revelation. In fellowship with him, however, it becomes a possibility for our own life too.

Let us now take verse 41 in addition: "If any one forces you to go one mile, go with him two miles." This verse offers very nearly something like a philological confirmation of the Christological interpretation of the sermon on the mount we are concerned about here. The Greek word translated here as "force" (ἀγγαρεύειν) is found in only one other context in the New Testament, in the account of the Passion (Mark 15:21, Matt. 27:32). There we are told that the soldiers "compelled" Simon of Cyrene to help Jesus carry his cross. This Greek word was a technical term from the Roman military vocabulary: it denotes the right of Roman soldiers to enlist civilians in certain cases for various auxiliary services, a kind of requisitioning.[18] This observation makes it clear how complex this saying of Jesus is. It can be read as a rejection of the Zealots, who refused that kind of service as collaboration with the enemy. In any case it includes the moral dimension of summoning us to help our neighbor more generously. But above all it bears within itself a Christological dimension: it challenges us to be a Simon of Cyrene on Jesus' way of the cross throughout all the centuries of history. It seems to me that here (regardless of exegetical arguments about the correctness and limits of such an interpretation) the real core of Christian *agape* comes to light, what of its nature it is: letting oneself be taken into service by the loving and suffering Christ, accepting being "requisitioned" by him for the least of the brethren in whom he is suffering, so as with him to bear the yoke of his "yes." In this kind of service, in going the second mile of his way, and only in this way, shall we finally discover that his yoke, apparently so heavy and oppressive, is in reality the burden of love that turns the yoke into wings. We shall discover that his saying is true: "My yoke is easy, and my burden is light" (Matt. 11:30).[19]

TWO SERMONS ON FAITH AND LOVE

"What Shall I Do to Inherit Eternal Life?"
A Homily on Luke 10:25–37

The conversation between Jesus and the lawyer deals with a question that affects all of us: How do I live properly? What must I do to succeed at being human? For this it is not enough to earn money and exert influence; one can be very rich and yet live in a way that misses the real point of living, that makes oneself and other people unhappy. One can be powerful and through this destroy more than build up. How then can I learn to be a human being? What belongs to this?

Already in his question the lawyer mentions a condition that usually we do not think of any more today: for this life to succeed I must in the midst of it set my sights on eternal life. I must think of the fact that God has a task in mind for me in the world and will ask me afterwards what I have done with my life. Today many people maintain that thinking about eternal life prevents people from doing the right thing in this world. But the opposite is true. If we lose sight of God's standard, the standard of eternity, then all that remains over as a guiding thread is nothing but egoism. We all will try to grab as much as possible out of this life for ourselves. We will see all the others as enemies of our happiness who threaten to take something away from us. Envy and greed take over the running of life and poison the world. If on the other hand we build our life in such a way that it can stand up in the sight of God, then it will make a glimmer of God's goodness visible for other people too. So a first rule is: don't live for yourself alone; live in the sight of God; live in such a way that he will be able to stand the sight of you and that eventually you will be able to be welcome in the company of God and his saints forever.

The lawyer's question thus really already includes the answer, which he himself then goes on to give. The way to the right kind of life runs: "You shall love the Lord your God with all your heart, and with all your soul, and with all your strength, and with all your mind; and your neighbor as yourself" (Luke 10:27). The first thing should thus be that God is present in our life. The sums of human life don't work out if God is left out: all that remains then is nothing but contradiction. So we mustn't just believe in some theoretical way that God exists: we must consider him to be the most important and real thing in our life. As Scripture says, he must penetrate every layer of our life and fill it completely: our heart must know about him and let itself be moved by him; our soul; the power of our will and decision; our intelligence. He must be everywhere. And our fundamental attitude towards him, our fundamental relationship to him, must be called love.

Often this can be very difficult. It can for example happen that someone is struck down with all sorts of illnesses and handicaps. Someone else's life is made intolerably difficult by poverty. Yet another loses those on whose love his or her whole life depended. There can be all sorts of unhappiness. Then the danger is very great that the person concerned becomes embittered and says: "God just cannot be good, otherwise he wouldn't be treating me like this. If God were to love me he would have created me differently and given me different qualities and made the circumstances of my life different."

This kind of revolt against God is very understandable. Often assent to God seems almost impossible. But those who abandon themselves to this rebellion poison their lives. The poison of negation, of anger against God and against the world, eats them away from within. But God wants from us as it were a down-payment of trust. He says to us: "I know you don't understand me yet. But trust me: believe me when I tell you I am good and dare to live on the basis of this trust. Then you will discover that behind your suffering, behind the difficulties of your life, a love is hiding. Then you will know that precisely in this way I have done something good for you." There are many examples of saints and great people who have dared to have this trust and who have thus found true happiness—for themselves and for many others—precisely in the greatest darkness.

Inner agreement with God thus belongs to the happy life. Only if this fundamental relationship is right can all the other relationships be right. For that reason it is important throughout one's life and from one's youth onwards to learn and to practice thinking with God, feeling with God, willing with God, so that love may grow from this and become the keynote of our life. If that is the case, love of neighbor becomes self-evident. For if the keynote of my life is love, then as far as concerns those whom God has placed on my way I can once again only live on the basis of this assent, this trust, this agreement, and this love.

To describe love of neighbor Holy Writ uses a very wise and profound phrase: "Love your neighbor as yourself." It does not demand any fantastic and unreal heroism. It does not say: "You must deny yourself and exist only for the other; you must make less of yourself and more of the other." No, it is as yourself: no more and no less. People who are dissatisfied with themselves will not be really good to others. Those who do not accept themselves take exception to others. True love is fair: where it is leading us is to love oneself as one of the members of

Christ's body. Oneself like the others—becoming free of that false perspective with which we are all born, as if the world revolves around me and my ego.

Through faith we must all learn a kind of Copernican revolution. Copernicus discovered that it was not the sun that went around the earth but that this earth along with the other planets revolved around the sun. We all begin by seeing ourselves as a tiny earth around which all the suns must turn. Faith teaches us to leave this error and to behave like brothers and sisters, joining together with all the others in the round dance of love around the one center that is God. Only if God exists, only if he becomes the center of my life, is this "love my neighbor as myself" possible. But if he exists, if he becomes my center, then it is also possible to reach this inward freedom of love.

The lawyer in today's gospel knew all this very well in theory. Why then did he put his question to our Lord? The gospel tells us that he wanted to put him to the test, and thus probably to embarrass him. But his second question showed that somewhere or other he was not himself happy with the relationship that theory and practice stood to each other in his life. There was in fact in his time—in the time of Jesus—a violent dispute over what the right practice of love of one's neighbor was. He clearly wanted to pin Jesus down in this dispute so as to lose him the sympathy of the other side. The whole thing was aimed at this, because the theoretical answers were not in dispute anyway. In this parable Jesus gave the answer to this dispute in the Israel of his time.

There was first of all the group of militant fighters for the kingdom of God, called Sicarii, who gathered around Judas the Galilean. They were guerrilla fighters who were trying to bring about the kingdom of God through armed struggle. One can assume that the robbers who fell on the man on the way from Jerusalem to Jericho were sicarii of this kind. For them violence was a means of love in order to bring about the future kingdom. Then there were the religious fanatics, the Zealots, who were pursuing the restoration of pure religion with all possible means, even violent ones. Common to these and other groups was the way they saw love in completely structural terms. According to them love is to change the world in such a way that it becomes the kingdom of God. With this maxim in their hearts they could cut others down or at least pass them by on the other side and leave them lying in the ditch. The Samaritan comes along without any theories. His heart tells him what love is: to help the person who needs me here and now with everything I have and can do; to treat that person as if that person were myself; to love that person as myself.

So Jesus' answer to the theoretical quarrel is very practical: love of one's neighbor must be literally that; its nature consists of my refusing to shift doing good into the future but doing what I can on the spot. Violence cannot be a means of love, nor indifference. Love must be fearless: perhaps quite apart from theories the priest and the Levite were simply afraid the same might happen to them, and so they hurried as fast as they could past the grim spot. The parable teaches us that it is not the big ideas that save the world but the courage to tackle what is at hand, the humility that follows the voice of the heart that is the voice of God.

The parable thus aims at awakening our heart so that we learn to see where our love is needed. When we simply talk about love of neighbor we are often involved in "biting and devouring one another" (Gal. 5:15). We quarrel about love, and this makes us incapable of perceiving what and who is at hand in need of that love. Let us pray to our Lord to awaken our heart again so that it can see. For it is only in this way that we shall grasp what it means to love our neighbor.

The Pure Vision and the Right Way:
A Sermon for the Feast of St. Henry

Today the Church celebrates the feast of St. Henry, who from 1002 to 1024 was emperor of the medieval Holy Roman Empire and thus the most powerful man of the Europe of his time. He was canonized because he placed his power at the service of what is true and what is good, because he recognized power to be a duty of service. So we can venerate him, but as a model from whom we can learn he seems hardly to come into question—the difference between the situation of his life and ours is too great. The problem most of us face is not how to cope with wielding power but coming to terms with our lack of it. And if he had to struggle to avoid letting himself be blinded by wealth, most Christians in most parts of the world are concerned about how in their poverty they can keep God in their view.

So to begin with this saint seems to be very far distant from us. But today's collect translates his life into a way that concerns us all. Our starting points are of course different, but ultimately the direction is the same. The collect as it were picks out the thread from a host of external events and thereby shows us all the way. Let us try to understand something of its guidance bit by bit.

First of all this prayer tells us that St. Henry was endowed with abundant grace. He was not what he had, what he was, from his own resources: it was given to him, it was grace, and for that reason it was also a responsibility he had to bear to God and to the others. Although our lives are built on quite different lines, the same applies to us too: everything essential in our lives has been given to us without our contributing to it. The fact that I am alive is not something I have derived from myself: the fact that people were there who introduced me to life, who enabled

me to experience love, who gave me faith and opened my
gaze to God—all that is grace. We could not do anything
if we had not been given the ability to do so first.

But at this point the questions start rising up within us.
Is God really fair with his gifts? Why does he give one
person so much and another so little? Why is everything
made so difficult for one person and everything pretty
well heaped up on another? If we burrow into questions
like this we do not get any closer to the truth. We just
don't know what goes on in somebody else's heart: we
know only tiny excerpts from the whole of reality and
thus argue very irrationally if on this basis we want to
judge the whole world. How, for example, would we be
able to know if power brought the Emperor Henry II
happiness? Could it not be that it was a fearful burden for
him in the immense decisions he was involved in? But we
can guess how heavily the fate of childlessness bore on a
soul, and historians have passed on to us how terribly he
suffered over many years from the pains his illness
brought him. In this way he too had to learn that God's
grace is often dark, but that it is precisely in suffering that
grace lies.

With grace we are dealing with something other: it
cannot be measured in the way that money can be
counted and possessions can be reckoned up. One must
learn to recognize it as grace in life and suffering, in daily
converse with God. God always precedes us with his

grace, and in every individual life there is something fine and good that we can easily recognize as grace, as the beam of light of divine goodness, if we only keep the eyes of our heart open. And if we do that, if we first of all have learned to recognize God in his goodness, then we can also learn to have trust in the dark ways that God always goes ahead of us as grace, that he means well towards us. So this saint could first of all invite us to have an eye for grace, for what is good, and to trust God even when we do not understand him.

In the next phrase the collect tells us that God has in a wonderful way raised the saint up to higher things from the cares of earthly rule. For the person praying it is already a kind of miracle if someone who is occupied with the care of an entire empire nevertheless notices that there is something higher and goes on to find the strength to pick himself up and look towards this higher thing.

But is it really so different with us? Does not the daily care of our life seem so important to us that we cannot find any time to look beyond this? There is the concern for our food and shelter for ourselves and for the people attached to us; our job, our work; there is the responsibility for society as a whole so that it becomes better, so that injustice ceases within it and so that all may be able to eat their bread in peace and freedom. Is this not so urgent that everything else seems trivial? Is this not the highest thing of all? More and more people are of the opinion today that religion is a waste of time and that only social action means really doing something for other people.

So today a kind of miracle is needed for us to be able to raise ourselves up towards what is higher. Thank God this miracle occurs even today. A friend who is a bishop told me that when he visited the Soviet Union he was told that today they estimate that in Russia 25 percent of the people are believers and 13 percent atheists: the rest, in other words the majority, are "seekers." Isn't this an exciting piece of news? Seventy years after the revolution that labelled religion as superfluous and harmful, 62 percent of the people are seekers who again are inwardly aware that there is something higher even if they do not know it yet. Earthly things only thrive if we do not forget what is higher. We should not lose the upright stance that distinguishes man. We should not look down: we must stand up straight, since only then do we live properly. We must remain on the quest for what is greater than us, and we must help those who struggle to stand up in order to find the true light without which everything in the world is darkness.

Finally the two statements in which the life of our saint is mirrored come together to conclude with a petition: may God give us what he was granted—to move, or rather hasten, towards God with a pure mind amid the changes of worldly things. Three elements should be noticed here. On the one hand is the multiplicity of earthly things. These are the cares and duties to which we are exposed every day from dawn to dusk and which so fill our mind and heart that they pursue us into our sleep. These include the flood of news that showers upon us, the images that remorselessly assail us, and all the ideas and opinions that the world forces upon us. The collect opposes to the oppressive power of this variety two other elements: a clear vision and single-minded progress. Both are not easy to attain. Who can look through and beyond the mass of experiences and images, of ideologies and dominant opinions? Who today can still hope to recognize what is right amid the ever-increasing mass of knowledge and the contradictions of specialists? Only God can give this to us, and for that reason this is a prayer to God in which everything else culminates. Only God can create a pure vision for us; only he can liberate us from the hopelessness of skepticism and grant us to see the truth through all the confusion. The pure vision is identical with the faith that tells us what is decisive and essential in the obscurity of the things of this world. But to keep the faith and so to see the right direction is today, as at all times, and perhaps more than in other times, a grace we must pray for.

The second petition for single-mindedly approaching God automatically arises from this. Faith becomes barren if it does not become life. It could well be that we receive the insight of faith but in the meantime want to keep our life as it was. In this way even faith can very quickly become forfeit. Faith is not something we can postpone until later. It is always here and now. That is why the collect says that we must hasten toward God. "Let nothing be put before the work of God," said St. Benedict when expressing this urgent quality of faith in his Rule. This too is not easy to accept for those assailed by the pressing cares of everyday life. This too must be prayed for: the quick, powerful step that will not be deflected from its goal.

If we had had to compose this collect ourselves we would probably have expressed other concerns: that we would succeed in this or that, that we would be spared the evil that threatens us, and other similar petitions. The Emperor Henry too would probably have of himself mentioned other concerns: that he might find the right decision in this affair, that he might succeed in overcoming resistance here, there in bringing a project to a successful conclusion, etc. All these concerns are justified: we should naturally bring them before God. They belong to the changing things of this world. They do indeed concern us, but they are not the only thing, nor are they the last. They should not monopolize us to the point of losing the clear vision, the vision for the truth that binds and unites us all, and the right step, the step that leads to God.

So this collect, through the figure of St. Henry, calls us to remember what is essential in our life. It summons us not to be submerged in what is separate and private but to look at the goal and thus at the same time to serve others. For every person who sees and does the truth helps other people and helps the whole of society. That God remains visible in the world and that the world remains in movement towards him in the most important and essential of all things, the presupposition of all other benefits. For this we wish to pray. Amen.

NOTES

Chapter I: Faith

1. On this see vol. 13 of the series edited by C. M. Schröder, *Die Religionen der Menschheit*; A. Bareau, W. Schubring, and C. von Fürer-Haimendorf, *Die Religionen Indiens III* (Stuttgart, 1964). On the relationship between Christianity and Buddhism, see H. Bürkle, *Einführung in die Theologie der Religionen* (Darmstadt, 1977), 63–92, where further literature is cited.

2. *Summa Theologiae* II–II, q. 10 a. 1 ad 1; see J. Pieper, *Lieben—hoffen—glauben* (Munich, 1986), 315 and 376.

3. *Pensées* 451.4 (Chevalier), 343 (Lafuma), 233 (Brunschvicg), 1215–16 of J. Chevalier's edition in the Bibliothèque de la Pléiade (Paris, 1954); on this see R. Guardini, *Pascal for Our Time* (New York, 1966), 138–72.

4. J. Pieper, *Lieben—hoffen—glauben*, 292 and 372, referring to J. H. Newman, *Grammar of Assent* (London, 1892), 342, and Aristotle, *Nicomachean Ethics* I:iv:7 (1095b), quoting Hesiod, *Works and Days* v. 293–96.

5. J. Pieper, *Lieben—hoffen—glauben*, 318; J. H. Newman, *Grammar of Assent* (London, 1892), 425–26.

6. See my Salzburg University address, "Konsequenzen des Schöpfungsglaubens" (Salzburg, 1980).

7. According to Pius XII, "the sin of the century is the loss of the sense of sin" (*Discorsi e Radiomessaggi* 7, 1946, 288 [radio message to the National Catechetical Congress of the U.S.A., Boston, October 26, 1946]). Pope John Paul II adds in his 1986 encyclical

Dominum et vivificantem 2:6 § 47: ". . . and this loss goes hand in hand
with the 'loss of the sense of God.'"

8. W. Jaeger, in *The Theology of the Early Greek Philosophers* (Oxford,
1947), has described the exciting drama of the rise and decline of
pre-Socratic philosophy, which after the great achievements of Par-
menides and Xenophanes ended with Democritus trying to deduce
religion from a deliberate political fiction: "God is the 'as if' that
serves to fill the gaps in the organization of the political system
already dominant" (188). For the subsequent period I would refer
readers to my book *Volk und Haus Gottes in Augustins Lehre von der Kirche*
(Munich, 1954), 265–76.

9. One should for example consider the logical structure of the
following remarks by J. Monod, *Chance and Necessity: An Essay on the
Natural Philosophy of Modern Biology* (London, 1972), 121: "If terres-
trial vertebrates appeared and were able to initiate the wonderful line
from which amphibians, reptiles, birds, and mammals later developed, it was originally because a primitive fish 'chose' to do some
exploring on land, where it could however only move about by
clumsy hops. This fish thereby created, as a consequence of a change
in behavior, the selective pressure that was to engender the powerful
limbs of the quadrupeds. Among the descendants of this daring
explorer, this Magellan of evolution, are some that can run at speeds
of fifty miles an hour. . . ." In such formulations, which characterize
the book's entire chapter on evolution, it is difficult to see anything
other than the self-mockery of the author who is convinced of the
absurdity of his argument but is bound to uphold it because of the
methodological stance he has decided to adopt. The mythical element is particularly obvious in R. Dawkins, *The Selfish Gene* (Oxford,
1976). On this see P. Koslowski, "Evolutionstheorie als Soziologie
und Bioökonomie. Eine Kritik ihres Totalitätsanspruchs," in
R. Spaemann, R. Löw, and P. Koslowski, *Evolutionismus und Christen-
tum, Civitas Resultate* (Weinheim, 1986), 9:29–56.

10. That is precisely the teaching of Vatican I on human knowledge of God; see especially the second chapter of the constitution *Dei Filius*, Denzinger-Schönmetzer 3004–7; see the contributions of R. Aubert (46–211) and G. Paradis (221–81) to the volume *De doctrina Concilii Vaticani Primi* (Vatican, 1969).

11. See the wonderful remarks about this text by Gregory of Nyssa in his *Vita Moysis*, culminating in the passage: "To the one searching for eternal life he [the Lord] prescribes: 'Come, follow me' (Luke 18:22). But the person who follows sees the rear [of the person being followed]. Moses, who desires to see God, is thus taught what it is to see God: to follow God wherever he may lead is to see God" (PG 44:408d). From here this interpretation entered into the spiritual tradition in a number of different variations, see, for example, in the Middle Ages William of St. Thierry, *De contemplando Deo* 3, ed. and trans. J. Hourlier, Sources chrétiennes 61 (Paris, 1959).

12. On St. Thomas's concept of theology see P. Wyser, *Theologie als Wissenschaft* (Salzburg/Leipzig, 1938); A. Patfoort, *St. Thomas d'Aquin: Les clefs d'une théologie* (FAC-éditions, 1983). On the problem at issue see my article "Theologie und Kirche" in *Internationale katholische Zeitschrift* 15 (1986), 515–33.

13. "Lumen fidei facit videre ea quae creduntur, *Summa Theologiae* II-II, q. 1 a. 4 ad 3; J. Pieper, *Lieben—hoffen—glauben*, 374.

14. There seems to me to exist a certain parallelism between John 1:18 ("No one has ever seen God; the only Son, who is in the bosom of the Father, he has made him known") and John 13:25 ("So lying thus, close to the breast of Jesus, he [the beloved disciple] said to him, 'Lord, who is it?'"), despite the difference of terminology (κόλπος in 1:18, στῆθος in 13:25) and contexts. The loving closeness of the disciple to Jesus corresponds to Jesus' intimacy with the Father, and, corresponding to Jesus' share in the Father's knowledge that makes him the one who reveals, the disciple too wins a share in Jesus' knowledge.

15. See my article "Theologie und Kirche" cited in note 12 above, especially 518–19. A helpful contribution is provided by R. Guardini, *Das Christusbild der paulinischen und johanneischen Schriften*, 2d ed. (Würzburg, 1961), 72–84.

16. On this see the fine remarks by R. Guardini, *Die Kirche des Herrn* (Würzburg, 1965), 59–70.

Chapter 2: Hope

1. See F. Hartl, *Der Begriff des Schöpferischen: Deutungsversuche der Dialektik durch Ernst Bloch und Franz von Baader* (Frankfurt-am-Main, 1979); G. Gutiérrez, *A Theology of Liberation* (Maryknoll, N.Y., 1973), especially 172–78. An important analysis of the difference between optimism and hope is to be found in J. Pieper, *Über das Ende der Zeit*, 3d ed. (Munich, 1980); see for example 85–86, where Pieper refers to J. Burckhardt's thesis according to which the conflict between the philosophy of life that emerged from the French Revolution and the Church, particularly the Catholic Church, exists throughout western Europe, a conflict that Burckhardt qualified more precisely as between optimism and pessimism. On this Pieper comments: "It may to some extent be accurate to label the philosophy of life of 1789 as 'optimism' (Burckhardt sees it characterized as a sense of acquisition and of power); although presumably a more penetrating analysis would have to come up against despair as the fundamental reason that makes this optimism possible. . . ."

2. See Pope John Paul II's 1986 encyclical on the Holy Spirit, *Dominum et vivificantem* II: 6 § 46; "And the blasphemy against the Holy Spirit consists precisely in the *radical refusal to accept this forgiveness*."

3. See on this my article "Gottes Kraft—unsere Hoffnung" in *Klerusblatt* 67 (1987), 342–47.

4. On the history of the prophet Jeremiah see J. Scharbert, *Die*

Propheten Israels (Cologne, 1967), 2:61–295, and the commentaries, most recently J. Schreiner, *Jeremia*, two volumes (Würzburg, 1981 and 1984). For the proper distinction and relationship of the different individual levels of reality in Christian hope see J. Ratzinger, *Politik und Erlösung* (Opladen, 1986).

5. See on this H. Schlier, *Besinnung auf das Neue Testament* (Freiburg-im-Breisgau, 1964), 358–73, and his *Das Ende der Zeit* (Freiburg-im-Breisgau, 1971), 67–84.

6. Matt. 7:26 and Rev. 12:18 use the same phrase, ἐπὶ τὴν ἄμμον. From a purely literary point of view this is of course a coincidence; nevertheless the connection does seem to me to be clear.

7. Detailed information on the present state of exegetical discussion on the interpretation of the sermon on the mount is provided by M. Hengel, "Zur matthäischen Bergpredigt und ihrem jüdischen Hintergrund," in *Theologische Rundschau* 52 (1987), 327–400. On the interpretation of the beatitudes see J. Gnilka, *Das Matthäusevangelium* (Freiburg-im-Breisgau, 1986), 1:115–32. The remarks of Cardinal J.-M. Lustiger on the beatitudes in his *Dare to Believe* (Slough, 1986), 103–8, are stimulating, drawing on modern philosophy and in many respects related to what is said here. The patristic insight that Jesus' parable must also be interpreted as evidence of his own method and work has been expounded again in our time by E. Biser (for example, *Die Gleichnisse Jesu* [Munich, 1965]), something which G. Baudler has then tried to incorporate in his "narrative theology" (most recently *Jesus im Spiegel seiner Gleichnisse* [Stuttgart/Munich, 1986]).

8. Augustine, *Contra Faustum* 11:7, PL 42:251; see Pieper, *Lieben—hoffen—glauben*, 212.

9. Bonaventure, sermon 16 for the first Sunday of Advent, *Opera*, 9:40a; see J. Ratzinger, "On Hope," *Communio*, Spring 1985, 71–84.

10. See on this J. Ratzinger, *Church, Ecumenism and Politics* (Slough, 1988), 237–54.

11. *Summa Theologiae* II-II, q. 17 a. 4; see J. Pieper, *Lieben—hoffen—glauben*, 213.

Chapter 3: Hope and Love

1. In what follows I follow closely Josef Pieper's treatment of hope in his book that I have already cited frequently, *Lieben—hoffen—glauben* (Munich, 1986), 189–254.

2. On this see my *Theologische Prinzipienlehre* (Munich, 1982), 78–87.

3. See R. Löw, "Die Unverzichtbarkeit des Naturbegriffs für die Moraltheologie" in *Weisheit Gottes—Weisheit der Welt: Festschrift für J. Ratzinger* (St. Ottilien, 1987), 1:157–77.

4. J. Pieper, *Lieben—hoffen—glauben*, 232–33.

5. *De malo* 11:4; J. Pieper, *Lieben—hoffen—glauben*, 232.

6. J. Pieper, *Lieben—hoffen—glauben*, 231.

7. These links are analyzed in a stimulating way through the figure of the Abbé Cénabre in Bernanos's novel *L'Imposture* (Bernanos, *Œuvres Romanesques* [Paris, 1961], 309–530). A few indications: "New feelings . . . sprang up together from a saturated soil. To his great surprise, the strongest among them was remarkably like hatred" (335). "It was an impersonal hatred, a burst of pure, essential hatred" (375). "'I think he doesn't love,' he said. 'He doesn't even love himself'" (363). A key element in the analysis of the reasons for this absolute hatred must make one think particularly today: the abbé came up against "his repugnance, his insuperable horror at the passion of Our Lord, the thought of which was always so painful to his nerves that involuntarily he turned his sight away from the crucifix" (364). This revulsion against our Lord's suffering has today indeed become one of the signs of the times. Seen from the perspective of today Bernanos's disturbing vision takes on a

prophetic clairvoyance. For an interpretation that needs to be taken up again today and continued see H. U. von Balthasar, *Gelebte Kirche*, 3d ed. (Einsiedeln/Trier, 1988), 339–43.

8. See J. Pieper, *Lieben—hoffen—glauben*, 237ff.

9. Bernanos portrayed this connection with biting irony in the figure of Bishop Espelette in the second part of *L'Imposture*. Bernanos describes the intellectual cowardice of this priest as boundless (387). "'I belong to my time,' he repeated.... But he had never considered that with that he was denying the eternal sign with which he was marked" (388).

The finest definition of the fear of God I found in a sermon by R. Guardini: "To fear God does not mean to be afraid of him but to experience in him the one who is holy; the unapproachable who is nevertheless close; the one who alone is real who bestows his fearful power on his own in grace. Hence above all shrink back from whatever is against him; but at the same time trust in him with a boundless trust beyond all earthly powers" (in *Wahrheit und Ordnung 3, Universitätspredigten* [Munich, 1955], 75: sermon on "The Living God," Psalm 113). Excellent texts on the fear of God are to be found in Diadochus of Photice, *Capita centum de perfectione spirituali*, Sources chrétiennes 5, 3d ed. (Paris, 1966), chap. 16 (92–93): "No one can love God in the perception of his heart unless first he fears him with all his heart; for it is through being cleansed and made tender, as it were, by the operation of fear that the soul comes to active love. Nor may anyone come fully to the fear of God in the way that has been mentioned unless he escapes from all the cares of this life; for when the mind attains great rest and freedom from care then the fear of God moves it and cleanses it in great perception from all earthly dullness so that in this way it may lead it to great love of the goodness of God." Chap. 17 (93–94): "Thus the soul, while it is uncared for and entirely covered by the leprosy of the love of pleasure, cannot perceive the fear of God.... But when it begins to be cleansed through great diligence, then it perceives the fear of God as being some medicine of life. . . ." Chap. 35 (104–5): "Just as when the sea is disturbed and oil is poured on it then, conquered by the richness of this, it shrinks back from storminess, so our soul, when it is enriched by the goodness of the Holy Spirit, becomes pleasantly calm. . . . This is the state someone reaches or remains in if he unceasingly sweetens his soul with the fear of God."

10. See M. Marmann, "Praeambula ad gratiam. Ideengeschichtliche Untersuchung über die Entstehung des Axioms 'gratia praesupponit naturam'" (dissertation, Regensburg, 1974); J. Ratzinger, "Gratia praesupponit naturam. Erwägungen über Sinn und Grenze eines scholastischen Axioms," in J. Ratzinger and H. Fries, *Einsicht und Glaube* (Freiburg-im-Breisgau, 1962), 135–49.

11. J. Pieper, *Lieben—hoffen—glauben*, 45. The following remarks follow to a considerable extent Pieper's masterly treatise on love.

12. My impression is that this is to be found in the later Karl Rahner, most consistently in *Foundations of Christian Faith: An Introduction to the Idea of Christianity* (London, 1978), 143: "The history of the world, then, means the history of salvation," and 146: ". . . when Christianity is interpreted exactly according to its own self-understanding it understands itself as the process by which the history of revelation reaches a quite definite and successful level of historical reflection, and by which this history comes to self-awareness historically and reflexively, a history which itself is coextensive with the whole history of the world." For a discussion of this see my *Theologische Prinzipienlehre* (Munich, 1982), 169–79.

13. For a more detailed treatment of this see my contribution "Vorfragen zu einer Theologie der Erlösung," in L. Scheffczyk, ed., *Erlösung und Emanzipation* (Freiburg-im-Breisgau, 1973), 141–55.

14. This example is taken from J. Pieper, *Lieben—hoffen—glauben*, 76; see also the vivid remarks on 73–80. In this context Pieper introduces the distinction between excusing and forgiving (75): "By

'excusing' is now to be understood minimizing and trivializing what is bad: I let something 'be okay' even though it is bad. . . ." In contrast: "One can only forgive something one explicitly regards as bad and the negativity of which one does not ignore at all. . . . On the other hand . . . forgiveness presupposes that the other person already condemns ('regrets') what he or she has done, and that moreover he or she accepts forgiveness." Important insights on this matter are provided by A. Görres, "Schuld und Schuldgefühle," in *Internationale katholische Zeitschrift* 13 (1984), 430–43.

15. See R. Guardini, *Die Annahme seiner selbst* (Mainz, 1987), 9–35; useful remarks are also to be found in W. K. Grossouw, *Biblische Frömmigkeit* (Munich, 1956), especially 61–96; see also my *Theologische Prinzipienlehre*, 82ff.

16. *Pensées* 736 (Chevalier), 739 (Lafuma), 553 (Brunschvicg), *Le mystère de Jésus*, ed. J. Chevalier, Bibliothèque de la Pléiade (Paris, 1954), 1313.

17. *The Adorable Heart of Jesus* I:5, used in the Office of Readings for August 19, the feast of St. John Eudes; see on this H. Bremond, *A Literary History of Religious Thought in France*, vol. 3, *The Triumph of Mysticism* (London, 1936), 497–572; F. Cayré, *Patrologie et histoire de la théologie*, 2d ed. (Paris, 1950), 3:81–85.

18. W. Bauer, *Wörterbuch zum Neuen Testament* (Berlin, 1958), s.v. ἀγγαρεύω; E. Schweizer, *The Good News According to Matthew* (London, 1976), 130.

19. On this see the wonderful remarks of Augustine in his sermon on the parable of the prodigal son (G. Morin, *S. Augustini sermones post Maurinos reperti* [Rome, 1930], S. Caillau II:11, 256–64): "He ran up to him and embraced him; that is, he put his arms round his neck. The arm of the Father is the Son: he enabled him to bear Christ, a burden that does not weigh down but lifts up. 'My yoke,' he says, 'is easy, and my burden is light.' He fell on one who was standing upright, and by falling on him prevented him from falling

again. So light is the burden of Christ that not only does it not oppress but it also lifts up. . . . It is good for you to bear it that you may be lifted up; if you were to put it down, you would be oppressed the more. . . . Perhaps some example can be found that will enable you to see physically what I am saying. . . . Notice this in the birds. Every bird bears its feathers. Do you think they are weighed down by them? Take the burden away, and they fall: the less of a burden the bird carries, the less does it fly. . . . So when the father fell on the neck of his son he lifted him up, he did not press him down; he honored him, he did not burden him. How then is a man fit for carrying God unless the God who is carried carries him?" (258–59).

PREFACE TO THE ORIGINAL EDITION

WHEN IN THE SUMMER of 1986 the founder of *Comunione e liberazione*, Mgr. Giussani, invited me to give a retreat at Collevalenza for the priests of this movement, there had just landed on my desk the volume in which Josef Pieper had brought together the essays he wrote in 1935, 1962, and 1971 on love, faith and hope in order to make them available to the public once again. This inspired me to devote the retreat to consideration of the three "divine virtues" and in doing so to use Pieper's philosophical meditations as a kind of textbook. This explains why, especially in the third chapter, the basic pattern of my reflections follows Pieper's presentation, to which I also owe a range of excellent quotations and references, especially from Thomas Aquinas. My own contribution has been to extend Pieper's philosophical presentation, which was devised within the framework of Christianity, into the theological and spiritual spheres.

I was at first hesitant over the pressure to publish this work, which came from those who took part in the retreat at Collevalenza. But when I had another look at the typescript two years later, it seemed to me that the linking of philosophy, theology, and spirituality that has resulted from the accidents of the work's preparation could perhaps be fruitful and open up new approaches. In translating it into German I have revised the text yet again but I have not wanted to blur its character of the spoken word and have deliberately left in references to the occasion for which these talks were first written. The aim was to keep what was direct and down to earth in what I said and to make possible fresh insights along these lines. To round off what perhaps remain all too fragmentary remarks about love I have included in this publication in book form two sermons I gave in Chile in the summer of 1988. I hope that this slim volume, which has come into being in this way, can serve, like the talks and sermons on which it is based, to help the practice of those fundamental attitudes in which human existence opens itself up to God and thus becomes truly human.

Rome
Ash Wednesday
JOSEPH CARDINAL RATZINGER

Of Related Interest

PPOPE JOHN PAUL II

HOLY FATHER, SACRED HEART

**The Wisdom of John Paul II
on the Greatest Catholic Devotion**

This treasury gathers together the complete writings of Pope John Paul II on the Sacred Heart of Jesus, with short commentaries by the editor, Fr. Carl Moell. Arranged by major theme, these readings are excellent for daily devotional reading and instruction.

0-8245-2147-1
$24.95 paperback

crossroad

Of Related Interest

POPE BENEDICT XVI

A NEW SONG FOR THE LORD
Faith and Christ in Liturgy Today

Not long ago, many people assumed that the goal of reforming the liturgy was to make it as accessible as possible. It is clear today that much more is at stake—liturgy is not just a pragmatic matter but a central feature in our relationship to Christ, the Church, and ourselves.

0-8245-1536-6
$19.95 paperback

At your bookstore or, to order directly from the publisher, please send check or money order (including $4.00 for the first book plus $1.00 for each additional book) to:

THE CROSSROAD PUBLISHING COMPANY
481 EIGHTH AVENUE, NEW YORK, NY 10001
1-800-707-0670 (toll free)

crossroad